# Political Speech as a Weapon

# Political Speech as a Weapon

## Microaggression in a Changing Racial and Ethnic Environment

Sylvia Gonzalez-Gorman

 PRAEGER™

An Imprint of ABC-CLIO, LLC

Santa Barbara, California • Denver, Colorado

**Library of Congress Cataloging-in-Publication Data**

Names: Gonzalez-Gorman, Sylvia, author.
Title: Political speech as a weapon : microaggression in a changing racial and ethnic environment / Sylvia Gonzalez-Gorman.
Description: Santa Barbara : Praeger, 2018. | Includes bibliographical references and index.
Identifiers: LCCN 2018019917 (print) | LCCN 2018036836 (ebook) | ISBN 9781440855832 (ebook) | ISBN 9781440855825 (alk. paper)
Subjects: LCSH: Communication in politics—United States. | Communication in politics—Psychological aspects. | Rhetoric—Social aspects—United States. | Race—Political aspects—United States. | Ethnicity—Political aspects—United States. | Microaggressions. | United States—Ethnic relations. | United States—Race relations. | United States—Politics and government.
Classification: LCC JA85.2.U6 (ebook) | LCC JA85.2.U6 G66 2018 (print) | DDC 320.97301/4—dc23
LC record available at https://lccn.loc.gov/2018019917

ISBN: 978-1-4408-5582-5 (print)
       978-1-4408-5583-2 (ebook)

22 21 20 19 18    1 2 3 4 5

This book is also available as an eBook.

Praeger
An Imprint of ABC-CLIO, LLC

ABC-CLIO, LLC
130 Cremona Drive, P.O. Box 1911
Santa Barbara, California 93116-1911
www.abc-clio.com

This book is printed on acid-free paper ∞

Manufactured in the United States of America

# Contents

# Acknowledgments

As with any project of this size, there are numerous people to thank and to whom I owe a great deal of gratitude—in an effort not to exclude any colleagues, friends, and family members, I say thank you to all and do not include individual names. I first got the idea for this book after a conversation I had with a colleague about race and the implications of changing demographics. My colleague and I would have in-depth conversations about race, religion, and anything politics. We would stop by each other's offices and would always have engaging conversations that left me with more questions and pondering the current political climate. I was introduced to literature on race that I was unfamiliar with, which started me down the political rhetoric path. I would like to thank my many colleagues for their guidance and patience as I asked a thousand questions about a topic that was not in my core area of research. As always, my colleagues were good listeners and willing to lend their guidance; for that I say thank you. As such, I would like to thank all of my other colleagues and friends who read iterations of this book and provided their feedback. You have all been a wonderful source to lean on when I questioned the enormity of this project.

I especially would like to thank my husband who has been patient and understanding as I worked on this project. My husband has never complained about my long hours at the computer or the fact that even when we traveled I would still mange to find time to "plug in" and work. I am grateful and forever indebted for his support and understanding. I would also like to thank Jessica Gribble with Praeger, ABC-CLIO, for her patience and guidance; I also thank the anonymous reviewers for their valuable comments and suggestions.

# Introduction

We can learn to see each other and see ourselves in each other and recognize that human beings are more alike than we are unalike.[1]

The 2016 U.S. presidential election was one of the most unconventional elections in modern times, and it left a lasting impression on me and a lot of other people. As a political scientist, I had family and friends constantly asking me: "Who is going to win the election?" "Can Hillary win?" "Is Trump going to pull it off?" "Are we going to have the first female president?" "This is hilarious—he's like Teflon, what are the chances he gets elected?" These are just some of the questions I fielded throughout the course of a long election. What made this election more interesting from a social science perspective was that there have not been many modern-day presidential elections where the candidates elicited outright vitriol and toxicity against each other to the point where voters were left wondering if these were adults or egocentric candidates out to destroy one another. The presidential field was large by prior standards; according to the Federal Election Commission, there were 17 Republican candidates, five Democratic candidates, one Libertarian, a Green Party candidate, and an independent all vying for the U.S. presidency.[2] It was one of the most diverse presidential elections to date. The candidates consisted of two women—one from each major political party—an African American, two Cuban Americans, an Irish American, and an Italian American, the first Indian American governor, and one of the oldest candidates—who appealed to millennials. Because the field was so diverse, most political pundits, including me, thought that some of the more boisterous candidates on both sides of the political aisle would eventually suspend their candidacies. But as the election moved along, the candidates that we assumed would not have enough support to sustain a viable campaign were drawing mega crowds to their political rallies.

As the election shifted and began to focus on the primaries, candidates from both the Republican and Democratic parties jostled for voters, and it struck me that one of the Republican candidates responsible for initiating the "birther movement" was a candidate for the highest and most powerful office in the world. On the Democratic side, you had a candidate who had a questionable political background and was being investigated by the Federal Bureau of Investigation (FBI). As the election shifted to the general election, these two remaining candidates were polar opposites. But what made this election even more fascinating to watch was the hostile political rhetoric that was being used by candidates on both sides of the political spectrum. The Democratic candidate called Republican supporters "deplorables," and the Republican candidate coined the phrase "crooked Hillary." Every word and movement from the two remaining candidates was watched and scrutinized by political pundits, the media, voters, and the rest of the world. But, more importantly, it was the hostile tone and the negative political rhetoric of the election that began to draw attention domestically and worldwide. The political rhetoric used in the 2016 presidential election, coupled with the multiple conversations I had with a colleague about race and ethnicity, were precipitating factors for this important project on the use of microaggressions in politics.

In this book, I examine the use of hostile political rhetoric by elected officials in local, state, and national politics. More specifically, I pay particular attention to the use of microaggressions in politics. During the 2016 presidential election the hostile political rhetoric laced with microaggressions seemed to be an anomaly—somehow un-American. While hostile political rhetoric that minimizes or degrades groups is not new to U.S. politics, very few people are aware of the long history of hostile political rhetoric that has been used to create divisiveness and a sense of "us against them." Some of the most lauded political figures in American history including Thomas Jefferson, Benjamin Franklin, and Abraham Lincoln have all engaged in microaggressive rhetoric. Jefferson used microaggressions to describe slaves, particularly the slaves he owned; Franklin engaged in microaggressions to describe Germans who had immigrated to the United States; and Lincoln, in his first senatorial debate with Douglas, was unequivocal about the hierarchical place of black men—a form of a microaggression. While certain microaggressions were common for this period and place in time, they should not be viewed as acceptable practices for elected officials or those in leadership positions. The examples of America's Founding Fathers' engaging in microaggressions provided in this book serve a larger purpose. They lay the foundation for the hostile political rhetoric that currently envelops our political system. In essence, the process of engaging in deliberate insults that minimize individuals or groups is not new.

If the use of hostile political rhetoric is not new in American politics, why should we care that microaggressions are used in politics? What makes the 2016 presidential election any different from previous elections? Does negative rhetoric really matter? The short answer is yes, it does matter. When rhetoric is used to create divisiveness and fear in society, it does matter. When microaggressions are used to insult and belittle women, people with disabilities, certain religions, Gold Star families, voters for the opposing party, and minority groups, we should all be concerned about the rhetoric our elected officials use. More importantly, recent data indicates that demographics are changing across the United States. If our elected officials are creating conditions where certain groups are perceived as inferior, we as citizens allow these conditions to continue by reelecting these individuals, and then we knowingly provide the opportunity for divisiveness, dissension, bigotry, and racism to flourish. As I argue throughout the book, negative political rhetoric, particularly microaggressions, matter in U.S. politics because this rhetoric is effective at creating an environment in which politicians and regular American citizens feel comfortable discriminating against certain people and groups, which leads to discriminatory public policy.

As a whole, it is no longer a white–African American dichotomy or racial divide. As the U.S. population has continued to grow, so have other minority groups like Latinos and Asian Americans. Minority groups such as African Americans, Asian Americans, and Latinos currently comprise a larger share of the U.S. population than compared to any other period in history. The demographics of the population is more ethnically and racially diverse, resulting in the United States becoming more multicultural and multilingual. Projections continue to indicate that there is a possibility of a demographic shift by 2060 where for the first time in history whites would constitute a minority population in the United States. As demographics continue to change, some elected officials may use this as an opportunity to engage in hostile political rhetoric and microaggressions as a way to create an "us against them" political environment.

This book examines how microaggression and its various forms are used to create hostile conditions for some groups, and how individual citizens gravitate toward the use of microaggressions and engage in their own microaggressive behavior. From shouting "Get out of my country" and "Make American great again" to the #MeToo movement that started in 2017, which exposed the sexual assault and harassment of women predominantly by elite males across all sectors of society, and the hope championed by elected officials that minority groups will begin to fight each other,[3] political rhetoric does matter. The danger of purposely categorizing certain groups into various segments of society by using microaggressions is that it opens the door for negative actions and reactions—both of which create divisiveness and an "us against them" political and social environment where one group is muted and the other elevated. This book also pays particular attention to President Trump's political rhetoric and its impact, and to the economic, social, and political conditions that result from Trump's rhetoric. Elected officials, the media, and scholars in a range of disciplines have all attempted to rationalize

Trump's election. Part of the rationalization process is figuring out why Trump continues to "get away with" his use of microaggressions and questionable behavior. The most commonly accepted theory is that citizens have become disillusioned with government[4] and with what government has to offer. I explore this theory and provide an alternative theory for why Trump continues to have support regardless of his actions.

This book makes three main points.

First, the use of microaggressions in modern-day politics is not new or a novel approach. History clearly demonstrates that elected officials who insult and belittle groups of people have always had supporters. Second, hostile political rhetoric does matter when it creates conditions where individuals act upon the negative rhetoric they hear from elected officials. Third, race and ethnicity are a factor in the use of microaggressions by elected officials. But more importantly, individuals self-select to overlook and/or minimize microaggressive actions of candidates and/or elected officials. For these individuals, toxic political rhetoric and negative behavior is what attracts them to a candidate. At an internal level, an individual makes the conscious decision to support a politician who espouses negative rhetoric and behavior that resonates with their own personal viewpoints, but outwardly these individuals try to hide or conceal their true feelings from others.

The sociopolitical idea of "us versus them" is not isolated to one group, race, religion, or political party—it is a factor that permeates every group, race, religion, and political party. Negative political rhetoric, particularly microaggressions, matter in U.S. politics because this rhetoric is effective at creating an environment in which politicians and regular American citizens feel comfortable discriminating against certain people and groups, which leads to discriminatory public policy. More troubling is the idea that an individual's use of toxic political rhetoric and negative behavior appeals to someone within our inner circle who shares our dinner table. This is why we should care about the rhetoric our elected officials use.

## The Rest of the Book

Chapter 1 discusses the use of microaggressions and how they are not a new phenomenon in education, employment, and politics. The chapter introduces the reader to what a microaggression is and their various forms, and how effective they are in denigrating individuals. Chapter 1 also examines how perpetrators frame microaggressions to convey superiority over an individual or group. The chapter provides up-to-date cases in which microaggressions were used by a perpetrator to intentionally hurt victims. Chapter 2 examines changing demographics and the possible shift of whites from majority to minority, and presents some of the challenges posed by changing demographics. It discusses why changing demographics matter, and then examines the political impact of growing minority groups. The chapter ends with a discussion on the difficulty of overcoming perceptions of race and microaggressions and the relapse back to Jim Crow.

Chapter 3 examines the use of inflammatory innuendos in American politics, and provides a historical perspective on how hostile political rhetoric is not new to American politics. It chronicles the use of hostile political rhetoric by the Founding Fathers and how microaggressions are often used as a weapon in changing racial and ethnic environments. Groups who have held the majority of elected positions may be uncomfortable with changing demographics, leading to the use of microaggressions. The chapter also presents interviews I conducted with elected officials at the local, state, and national level who have encountered microaggressions in their roles as elected officials. Local officials were more likely to push back against microaggressions when compared to individuals elected at the state and national level.

Chapter 4 explores growing nativist sentiment across the United States since the election of Donald Trump. The chapter examines the motivation and theoretical ecology of nativism in the form of hate crimes and the social constructs of hate crimes. It chronicles instances where African Americans, Asians Americans, Latinos, and other minority groups have been targets of violent attacks because of their race or religion. The chapter highlights how elected officials use their platforms to engage in various forms of microaggressions.

Chapter 5 explores the realization that times are changing. These changes translate into variations in race and ethnicity, cultures, religions, and public policy. This chapter examines issues such as economic, political, and social inequality as part of a larger discussion about the hierarchical status of minorities in America and the extent to which minorities will define future public policies and political debate. It presents a discussion on how political microaggressions are akin to Pandora's box: while insults and hostile rhetoric allow individuals and political elites to define the political landscape, the effects provide a platform for nativists, extremists, and hate groups to portray certain groups as threatening by insisting they are only saying what everyone else is thinking or doing what everyone wishes they could do. The chapter seeks to examine what Americanism is and what it means to be an American. Data is provided to show that while demographics continue to change, the American spirit is still thriving and people are more accepting of others than one might expect.

Chapter 6 examines the Trump effect and why he continues to "get away with" using microaggressions and demonstrating poor behavior. The chapter presents several theories for why Trump was elected and why he continues to use hostile political rhetoric. It also investigates why now is the time in American history that we feel comfortable electing a president who uses microaggressions on a daily basis. It also presents a new theoretical concept—the imperceptive panacea influence—that seeks to provide a rationale for why some individuals continue to support Trump regardless of his use of micro-aggressions. This chapter also provides an analysis of several former and current elected officials who have rejected Trump's use of political microaggressions and instead urge everyday citizens to become civically engaged and to reject nativism and bigotry coming from the highest levels of government.

In the concluding chapter, Chapter 7, I examine the transformation process and the challenges ahead in an unconventional political era. This chapter asks readers to consider whether Trump's microaggressions are any different from those of Thomas Jefferson, who wrote that blacks were inferior to whites; Benjamin Franklin, who compared Germans to swarming hogs; or Abraham Lincoln stating that he belonged to the superior race in his debate with Stephen A. Douglas. It also questions why Americans have become tolerant of microaggressions in political rhetoric, which under any other circumstances they would equate to bullying and would not tolerate.

# CHAPTER ONE

# Subtle Yet Effective: Microaggression Cues

During the 2016 Republican National Convention, legendary Notre Dame college football coach Lou Holtz offered his views on immigration at a luncheon hosted by the Republican National Coalition for Life. Holtz compared immigrants to an "invasion," stating that immigrants coming to the United States should learn to speak English and "become us." Holtz went on to say, "I don't want to become you." "I don't want to speak your language, I don't want to celebrate your holidays, I sure as hell don't want to cheer for your soccer team!"[1]

The use of microaggressions is not a new phenomenon in education, employment, and politics. What is new is the format in which microaggressions are communicated. In a technological era where cable television, social media, and the Internet are accessible 24/7, an avenue has been created in which perpetrators of microaggressions are free to espouse their comments with little oversight. On the other side, recipients of microaggressions are also impacted by *their* use of technology. This group is exposed to microaggression messages via the same medium that perpetrators use (i.e., cable television, social media, and the Internet). The term *racial microaggression* was introduced in 1970 and defined as everyday subtle verbal and nonverbal attacks and insults directed toward others, generally African Americans.[2] Racial microaggressions are systematic forms of racism used to "keep those at the racial margins in their place."[3] Microaggressions are typically unconscious views of inclusion/exclusion and superiority/inferiority negatively impacting the recipient.[4] However, microaggressions can also be intentional due to feelings of superiority from perpetrators. Take, for example, legendary coach Lou Holtz from the vignette above. Holtz intentionally conveyed various microaggressions against immigrants, validating his own implicit superiority by stating, "I don't want to become you. . . . I don't want to speak your language, I don't want to celebrate your holidays, I sure as hell don't want to cheer for your soccer team!"[5] Holtz's outburst is a classic example of a microaggression, an intentional insult meant to demean others.

This chapter will introduce readers to racial and political microaggressions in politics. It also asks why we should care that microaggressions are used in politics and whether negative political rhetoric really matters. The short answer is yes, we should care. Negative political rhetoric, particularly microaggressions, matter not only in society in general but also in U.S. politics. Negative rhetoric is effective at creating an atmosphere where politicians and regular Americans citizens feel comfortable disparaging and stereotyping certain individuals and groups, which leads to an inequitable sociopolitical environment. While political microaggressions are the focus of this book, it is important to acknowledge that microaggressions are not isolated to political venues; they are part of everyday life for many recipients of microaggressions and their perpetrators. This chapter will briefly acquaint readers with microaggressions in education and employment as a way to provide a complete picture on the use of microaggressions in society.

The majority of research on racial microaggressions derives from the discipline of psychology, which provides a contextual framework for what constitutes a microaggression.[6] Derald Wing Sue and colleagues define racial microaggressions as commonplace, intentional or unintentional, verbal and nonverbal demeaning comments that communicate hostile, derogatory, or negative insults toward a person or group.[7] Examples of microaggressions include the assumption that all Muslims are terrorists; a white man or woman crossing the street or clutching their bag or purse when they see an African American or Latino man approaching; the assumption that all Asians are good at math and science;[8] commenting that all Latinos must have swum over (alluding to swimming across the Rio Grande River to reach the United States), and the assumption that all Latinos are of Mexican descent and undocumented. Although prior scholarship and research contends that microaggressions are often unintentional, blatant incidents of derogatory or negative insults routinely erupt, resulting in recipients being offended and perpetrators arguing that society has become too politically correct.

Perpetrators frame microaggressions in two distinct ways: first, as harmless, inoffensive, and often as nonracially motivated,[9] and second, as intentional insults that can be racially motivated, which communicate feelings of inferiority and superiority among individuals. Research shows that overt forms of racism such as cross burnings have changed to less obvious forms of biases that often occur outside the consciousness of well-intentioned individuals.[10] In his research on microaggression, Derald Wing Sue found that white Americans are socialized to internalize their biases, stereotypes, and prejudices.[11] More recent research also indicates that perpetrators of micro-aggressions are not aware of the impact their actions have on minorities.[12] Although prior scholarship has laid a strong foundation for the notion that microaggressions are unconscious and oblivious actions, the contribution of this research puts forth the argument that microaggressions are intentional and purposeful and provide perpetrators an avenue for expressing internalized biases. Lou Holtz, a celebrated college football coach and the grandson of immigrants, used microaggressions as a release for his internalized stereotypes and prejudices against immigrants. Individuals may be more aware than we think about what they say, how they behave, and the stereotypes, biases, and prejudices they hold.

Microaggressions are used daily to insult and minimize individuals or groups; common examples of everyday microaggressions are illustrated in the following vignettes. An interracial couple invite the husband's mother to lunch after Sunday church. During the lunch, the mother-in-law makes a derogatory comment about Mexicans—the wife, who is Latina, exchanges "a look" with her husband. The mother-in-law, who is white, notices the exchange, leans over and touches the wife's hand, and says "Oh, but you're not like them." In another instance, another interracial couple invite the husband's father to lunch. On the way to lunch, the group is visiting with each other and the father-in-law, who is white, mentions that he has a friend who is Puerto Rican. The father-in-law then states, "I call him a Mexican just to tease him . . . he gets mad at me and tells me he's Puerto Rican, not Mexican. I just laugh and say that he just had to swim farther to get here." On the other hand, take for example, the following tweet from U.S. president Donald Trump intentionally disparaging a U.S. Congressman:

> Little Adam Schiff, who is desperate to run for higher office, is one of the biggest liars and leakers in Washington, right up there with Comey, Warner, Brennan and Clapper! Adam leaves closed committee hearings to illegally leak confidential information. Must be stopped.[13]

As can be seen from these intentional comments, microaggressions are recurrent, continuous, and unending.[14] As microaggressions build up, any one may represent the "last straw" that elicits an unexpected and intense reaction from the recipient.[15] As such, perpetrators may not be as benign in their microaggressive behavior as previously thought. Why does this type of rhetoric matter? Because negative political rhetoric, particularly microaggression, is effective at creating a divisive environment where politicians and regular Americans citizens feel comfortable denigrating certain individuals and groups, which leads to inequitable sociopolitical policies and conditions.

## What Is a Microaggression?

Most analyses on microaggressions are linked to race—the inclusion, exclusion, superiority, and inferiority of a specific group—meaning that an individual will be targeted for microagression based on his or her race. However, this book extends the conceptualization of microaggressions to include political rhetoric.[16] The framework of microaggressions has much to offer the political arena; the use of hostile political rhetoric by some elected officials and candidates is entwined with microaggressions, resulting in political polarization and an "us versus them" political and social environment. For these purposes, the theoretical framework I offer for political microaggressions is rooted in the constructs and taxonomy of psychology and extends the meaning of microaggressions to the following: political microaggressions are direct, intentional, verbal, and divisive comments that communicate hostile, derogatory, or negative insults toward a person, group, or organization. Elected officials and/or candidates at various levels of government engage in negative political rhetoric to rally supporters while at the same time deliberately ostracizing a person, group, or organization. Political microaggressions target political opponents, political colleagues, voters, women, men, minorities, LGBT people, military veterans, immigrants, religious groups, and those with disabilities. Political rhetoric that marginalizes these groups conveys the message that these groups are less desirable and that it is acceptable for members of society to perceive them negatively.[17]

Moreover, the field of psychology identifies three forms of microaggressions that are also used in conjunction with political microaggressions: microassaults, microinsults, and microinvalidation. These forms of microaggressions convey a deliberate or inadvertent disparaging remark toward a person or group. Political rhetoric is often infused with one or all three forms of these microaggressions. More importantly, political rhetoric based on microaggressions does influence how people act and react to hostile political rhetoric.

With this in mind, microaggressions are delineated in the following manner: *microassaults* are often-conscious, intentional biased beliefs or attitudes that are expressed primarily by a violent verbal or nonverbal attack meant to hurt a marginalized person or group.[18] Microassaults are characterized by name-calling, persistent discriminatory actions, and avoidant behavior.[19] A microassault equates to "old-fashioned racism" where the action is conscious and deliberate.[20] Take for example Adam W. Purinton, who on February 24, 2017, shot and killed Srinivas Kuchibhotla, a legally authorized immigrant from India, at a sports bar in Kansas City, Missouri. Witnesses indicated that Purinton shouted racial slurs and "Get out of my country" at the victim before firing and killing Kuchibhotla.[21] In this microassault case, Purinton held a biased belief about immigrants and acted on those beliefs. More significant, Purinton expressed his bias by shouting "Get out of my country."

A *microinsult* is often unconscious behavior or a verbal remark that is disguised as a compliment or positive statement directed toward the target group or person.[22] An example of a microinsult occurred when Joe Biden, then the senator from Delaware, made a controversial comment about then senator of Illinois, Barack Obama. Biden was quoted as saying "I mean, you got the first mainstream African-American who is articulate and bright and clean and a nice-looking guy. I mean, that's a storybook, man."[23] Here the emphasis is on "first mainstream," as if all other African Americans were not mainstream, bright, clean, or nice looking: a compliment infused with a subtle insult. Similarly, consider a news conference with President Trump and April Ryan, an African American White House correspondent and bureau chief of American Urban Radio. Ryan, in her normal duties as a White House correspondent, asked President Trump if he would be meeting with the Congressional Black Caucus (CBC) to discuss his urban agenda. Trump in his response asked Ms. Ryan to set up a meeting with members of the CBC; he then further asked if the CBC were her friends. The assumption was that because Ryan is an African American, she must know the members of the CBC. In this case, Trump attempts to make a positive statement about setting up a meeting with the CBC, but his comments reveal an unconscious microinsult in which he assumes all African Americans must know each other.

*Microinvalidations* are often unconscious and occur outside the awareness of a perpetrator; this form of microaggression is the most damaging because verbal comments or behaviors negate or nullify the thoughts and feelings of people of color.[24] For instance, Asian Americans and Latinos are often perceived as being foreigners in the United States; these groups are often told, "You are not an American" or "If you don't like it here, then go back." There is an implied assumption that Asian Americans and Latinos have an allegiance to another country, not the United States.[25] The constructs of microinvalidations are rooted in race because they disagree with or do not acknowledge the realities of minorities.[26] Many microinvalidations stem from institutional microaggressions where people of color are confronted with microaggressions in government, education, employment,[27] and through political rhetoric. The negative effects from these forms of microaggressions vary by individual, group, and organization. Regardless of the form of microaggression (the damaging effects from microaggressions vary), these negative cues conveyed by political elites suggest certain social group identities are inferior and insignificant.[28]

## Microaggressions in Education and Employment Settings

While the majority of this book will focus on microaggressions in political rhetoric, it is worthwhile to examine how microaggressions play out in settings outside of politics. It is also important to illustrate that perpetrators of microaggressions are not isolated to elected officials; microaggressive behavior is rampant in commonplace education and employment settings. Thus, the unconscious views of inclusion, exclusion, superiority, and/or inferiority that negatively affect recipients are not limited to race; the use of microaggressions is also prevalent in institutional settings such as education.[29] For instance, although microaggressions are often unintentional, institutions (i.e., educational settings) often create environments where microaggressions are routinely communicated to students. Educational institutions sometimes create environments that communicate negative cues to students about their academic capabilities.[30] Preconceived stereotypes set the stage for how students interact with educators. For example, educators with preconceived racialized assumptions about male African American middle-class students had negative assumptions regarding student intelligence.[31] Intentional or unintentional preconceived racialized assumptions create an atmosphere in the classroom that is noninclusive to all students. Take for example, a high school advanced placement U.S. government teacher who referred to undocumented immigrants from Mexico as "wetbacks" in her lecture to students. The high school teacher may or may not be aware of her bias or preconceived attitude toward immigrants from Mexico or Latinos in general. In one statement, the high school teacher nullified the fact that not all immigrants are from Mexico or undocumented. Microaggressions, particularly by educators, matter because they create a hostile learning environment for students. One of the most influential socialization processes is between educators and their students[32]—more significant, negative rhetoric in the classroom can influence how students view and interact with each other.

From the perspective of people of color, microaggressions are obvious and implied insults that convey a demeaning message.[33] To illustrate the point, consider the interaction between an American Latino college student and his college professor:

> As part of my undergraduate degree plan, I was required to take a foreign language in order to graduate. Somehow, I managed to CLEP [College Level Examination Program] out of four hours of Spanish, but still needed to take one more Spanish course. Spanish was difficult for me since English was my first language, but I decided to take the second part of intro Spanish. During the course of the semester, I struggled with the grammar, and one day after class, I decided to go to my professor's office hours and ask for some help. When I got to his office there was a line of students waiting, and when I finally walked into his office and introduced myself, he just looked and me and said, "Are you Hispanic?" I just looked at him and said "Yeah." My professor kept staring at me, and in a condescending voice said, "But you don't have an accent when you speak and how can you be struggling in my class? You just need to study harder." I just looked at

him and said, "Don't talk to me that way, I don't need your help" and walked out of his office. I was so angry and to this day, it still makes my blood boil.[34]

In the above exchange, the college professor intentionally insults the student by expressing his surprise that the student does not speak with an accent and is struggling with the course. The professor had a preconceived stereotype about Latino students, which illustrates how his disparaging remarks still impact the student. The microinvalidation is occurring outside the awareness of the professor and is the most damaging because verbal comments or behaviors negate the student. This is another example of why microaggressions matter in education. A hostile environment was created marginalizing and ostracizing the student.

Student-to-student microaggressions are also prevalent in academic spaces. Microaggressions between students create a hostile climate for the student who is attacked. Take this account from a female graduate student at a major university in the Southwest. She provides this account of her personal experience with a male colleague over graduate stipends.

Bill and I, both first-year graduate students, were catching up on homework in the graduate lab when Bill asked me if I had received my stipend award letter for the upcoming school year. Bill tells me that he has received his letter and has been denied funding. I was concerned about my funding status, so I stepped out of the grad lab to check my student mailbox in the department office. Upon reading my letter, I realized I had been funded for the next school year, so I went back to the lab. Bill was anxious to learn what my funding status was, and he asked me if I was awarded funding. For a minute, I thought about whether or not I should be honest with Bill about my funding. I decided to let him know I was awarded a stipend.

Bill was in shock that I had been awarded a stipend and he says to me "The only reason you received funding is because you are the token female and minority in the first-year cohort." In disbelief over what I had just heard, I asked Bill if he was serious and if he truly believed my funding was because of my gender and ethnicity. Bill responded, "Yes, I'm the work mule for everyone to step on just because I'm white." I then decided to confront Bill about his comments and asked him if he thought grades had anything to do with students getting funding. Bill, caught completely off guard by the question, says "But, my grades are better than yours." At this point, I knew my grades were higher than Bill's and asked him to reveal his grades. As we compared grades, Bill was shocked to learn that my grades were much better than his and he said, "I didn't think you were smarter than me." I simply said, "Well, I am" and turned my back to Bill and continued working on my homework.[35]

Microinvalidations are often unconscious and occur outside the awareness of a perpetrator—this brief account reveals that it never occurred to Bill that graduate funding was based on grades and not gender or race.[36] Instead, Bill was sure his microaggressive preconceived stereotypic assumptions of minority female students as "tokens" was the only reason he had not received funding.[37] As demographics continue to change in the United States, diversity in education will also continue to increase. Thus, the use of microaggressions in educational settings has the potential to increase stress in already stressful environments, leaving underrepresented students to deal with the insult, anger, and feelings of isolation.

Microaggressions are not limited in their reach. Microinsults, microassaults, and microinvalidation attacks can manifest in multiple settings. Microaggressions are also prevalent in the workforce.[38] Because microaggressions are brief, commonplace verbal, behavioral, and environmental insults, they are often ambiguous and subtle; thus, individuals may perceive microaggressions in the workforce differently depending on the contextual environment.[39] Internalized biases and stereotypes about certain groups can lead to inflated views about one's superiority and the inferiority of others.[40] In some work environments, evaluations used to measure and manage performance can often disguise unintentional microaggressions. For example, employees of color, certain genders, and those with disabilities often receive feedback such as "Everyone can succeed in this company, if they work hard enough" or "I believe the most qualified person should get the job."[41] Comments such as these send a message that some groups are lazy or incompetent and that some employees are given an unfair advantage because of their group identification.

Because microaggression cues are often unintentional, perpetrators are often unaware that their comments are off-putting and insulting. Take for instance, the exchange between a financial service manager and a member of her staff. In this exchange, the manager is speaking with one of her staff members who is a native of a country outside the United States. In the exchange, the manager, who is standing over the employee, states in a loud voice: "What language are you speaking? Is that even English?" At this organization, employees work in cubicles with very low walls, and thus other employees can hear and see the interaction between the two individuals. The employee whose language skills are being questioned is visibly uncomfortable, and her face turns red from embarrassment. Moreover, other employees who are witnessing the exchange are also uncomfortable with what the manager has said. After several more comments about the employee's language skills, the manager walks away from the area, leaving the witnesses deflated, embarrassed, and angry. The employee who bore the brunt of the exchange is also embarrassed and comments to her coworker, "Why is she so mean?" Throughout this exchange, the manager was unaware that she had exhibited classic signs of microaggressions and microinvalidations toward underrepresented minority employees.

Although overt, denigrating remarks are often seen as harmless, inoffensive, and nonracially motivated, they create negative and hostile environments for the affected employees.[42] Moreover, overt racial microaggressions often take place between supervisors and trainees. Recent research by Madonna G. Constantine and Derald Wing Sue on cross-racial supervisory relationships between white supervisors and African American doctoral students in counseling and clinical psychology programs found numerous microaggression offenses directed at African Americans.[43] The cross-racial supervisory study found that white supervisors in clinical settings often made stereotypic assumptions about African American clients and their trainees. Several trainees reported that their supervisor made comments such as "You shouldn't expect a lot of African American clients" and "I know that black people sometimes have a different time orientation and think it's okay to be late for stuff, but I don't want this to turn into some kind of cultural thing. Just get here on time."[44] Because microaggressions are cumulative, the damaging effects from microaggressions vary from continued stereotypic views to cues that suggest certain social group identities are less worthy.[45] Internalized biases and stereotypes about certain groups can lead to negative working conditions for recipients of microaggressions.

Without doubt, microaggressions are present in various public and private settings. Although some microaggressions occur outside the consciousness of some perpetrators, there are numerous other hostile behaviors or verbal comments that purposely occur with the intent of marginalizing certain individuals or groups. As such, microaggressions in education and in the workplace create polarizing conditions where recipients have little to no power. Recipients are devalued and remain isolated because institutional microaggressions are difficult to explain and prove.[46]

Up to this point, the taxonomy on microaggression has been defined and its prevalence illustrated in education and employment settings. With this foundation of what microaggressions are and how contextual factors matter, the remainder of the book will discuss the role of political microaggressions and their role in cuing supporters while denigrating others, and how microaggressions intersect with other issues, creating a polarizing economic, political, and social environment.

## Political Environment

In most instances perpetrators of microaggressions are unaware that they have spoken or acted in a demeaning manner.[47] However, in today's political climate these subtle, hidden messages are no longer subtle; this research argues that some comments are now direct, intentional hostile attacks.

Political speech laced with microaggression cues is used as a weapon in a changing racial and ethnic environment. While this work acknowledges that the overall effect of microaggressions is difficult to measure, the focus will be on the use of microaggressions in U.S. politics at various levels of government. Microaggressions are not new; since the founding of the United States they have been regularly utilized and have become part of normal political discourse in the political arena. The Founding Fathers were perpetrators of microaggressions, creating an economic, political, and social trajectory that emphasized an "us versus them" system.

In American politics, microaggressions do not exist in a vacuum—both Republican and Democratic candidates and elected officials have been perpetrators of political microaggressions. As an illustration, in 2013, U.S. Congressman Charlie Rangel (D-NY) created an uproar for his use of a racial microaggression when he compared members of the Tea Party to "White Crackers and racists." Rangel's remarks created an opportunity for Republicans to argue that Democrats are just as guilty as Republicans in creating racial divides. Similarly, in a speech to supporters, Dick Harpootlian, former chairman of the South Carolina Democratic Party, made disparaging remarks about then South Carolina governor Nikki Haley, the first female and Indian American governor of the state. Harpootlian told supporters he "hoped her political challenger would send her back to wherever the hell she came from."[48] Harpootlian later qualified his comments by stating he meant that Haley should "go back to being an accountant in a dress store rather than being this fraud of a governor that we have."[49] By no means are these the only elected officials and/or candidates who have used microassaults to negatively frame individuals and groups. There is a long-documented history in the United States of political elites using hostile rhetoric to rally supporters and create societal divisions—beginning with the Founding Fathers, which will be explored in Chapter 3.

The political elite's use of intended or unintended verbal insults, snubs, discriminatory remarks, or actions that result in bias plays a negative role in how citizens view and interact with each other. Recall from the discussion above political microaggressions are:

> direct, intentional, verbal, and divisive comments that communicate hostile, derogatory, or negative insults towards a person, group, or organization. Elected officials and (or) candidates at all various levels of government engage in negative political rhetoric to rally supporters while at the same time deliberately excluding a person, group, or organization. Political microaggressions target and marginalize numerous groups (e.g., political opponents, political colleagues, voters, women, men, minorities, LGBT people, military veterans, immigrants, religious groups, and those with disabilities), conveying the message that these groups are less desirable and that it is acceptable for members of society to perceive them negatively.

For example, in the 2016 U.S. presidential election, the issue of immigration once again catapulted to the forefront of public scrutiny. Republican presidential candidate Donald Trump made headlines with inflammatory comments comparing illegal immigrants to "rapists and killers." Following his remarks, in August 2015 Scott and Steve Leader, brothers from South Boston, violently ambushed a homeless Latino man (who was a U.S. citizen from birth). Police indicated that one of the brothers cited Trump's stance on immigration as motivation for the attack. In 2016, in a similar instance in West Texas, a native Pakistani physician of hematology was shopping at a local WalMart with his wife when a white man approached the physician, yelling "Get out of my country, make America great again."[50] The comment reflected Donald Trump's campaign slogan of "Make America Great Again" in the 2016 U.S. presidential election. What makes these interactions powerful is that the behavior and rhetoric in these two instances are directly tied to the rhetoric in the 2016 U.S. presidential election. Both events were fueled by a microassault communicated by a political elite, followed by a nativist racial reaction.

In a similar instance, Hillary Clinton, the democratic presidential nominee in the 2016 U.S. presidential campaign, was quoted at a New York fundraiser comparing her rival Donald Trump's supporters to deplorables:

> To just be grossly generalist, you could put half of Trump's supporters into what I call the basket of deplorables. Right? [Laughter/applause]. The racist, sexist, homophobic, xenophobic, Islamophobic—you name it. And unfortunately, there are people like that, and he has lifted them up. He has given voice to their websites that used to only have 11,000 people, now have 11 million. He tweets and retweets offensive, hateful, mean-spirited rhetoric. Now some of those folks, they are irredeemable, but thankfully they are not America.[51]

Microinvalidations often target people of color; however, Clinton's comments negated and invalidated some Trump supporters. Although this was an unusually vitriolic election, many Trump supporters were framed as racist nativists, with little to no education. Arlie Russell Hochschild, a professor of sociology at the University of California, Berkeley, spent five years interviewing Trump supporters in Louisiana about government and the role of government. Professor Hochschild found that many Trump supporters felt like strangers in their own land—they had become another minority group that no one was paying attention to.[52] Clinton's use of the term "deplorable" reaffirmed the microinvalidation that some Trump supporters already knew existed. Negative political rhetoric, especially microaggressions, matter in U.S. politics because this rhetoric creates an atmosphere where politicians and regular American citizens feel comfortable discriminating against each other, which leads to discriminatory socioeconomic policies.

Studies show dominant groups will use microaggressions when they can benefit politically, economically, and socially by manipulating differences between groups, while simultaneously using their power to portray subordinate groups as unambitious and threatening.[53] Political elites use political microaggressions intentionally and unintentionally to create a vacuum that appeals to voters. Political microaggressions are not mainstream, yet the message is appealing to those voters who feel disconnected from politicians and politics. The paradoxical effect of political microaggressions is one in which negative and hostile rhetoric resonates with some individuals while at the same time ostracizing others.

## Framing

Framing is an "organizing idea or storyline that provides meaning to an unfolding strip of events, weaving a connection among them. The frame suggests what the controversy is about, the essence of the issue."[54] Frames provide more than "positions or arguments about an issue—they spell out the essence of the problem."[55] Framing suggests how issues should be examined and how they should be dealt with if needed,[56] and can draw attention to certain aspects of a message, which can influence how individuals perceive an issue.[57] How information or arguments are framed and communicated (facts versus disinformation) can influence how individuals evaluate an issue. In other words, how an issue is framed can be effective in eliciting individual responses. In addition, several studies show that for framing to be effective, some of the facts have to be altered.[58] As Thomas Nelson and Donald Kinder argue, frames filter into our discussions of politics; framing teaches an average citizen how to grasp and comprehend multifaceted public policy problems:[59]

> When frames suggest what the essence of an issue is, they provide a kind of mental recipe for preparing an opinion. Citizens are almost always in possession of a variety of considerations that might all plausibly bear on any particular issue.[60]

As an illustration of framing to create a blurred picture, Representative Bennie Thompson (D-MS), in a wide-ranging radio interview on the topic of affirmative action and the Supreme Court, referred to Justice Clarence Thomas as an "Uncle Tom," a derogatory term for a subservient person of color.[61] Thompson went on to say of Justice Thomas, "It's almost to the point saying this man doesn't like black people, he doesn't like being black."[62] This was an example of a microinvalidation from an individual in the same racial group. Justice Thomas was framed as being subservient to the other justices and as someone who is uncomfortable as an African American, blurring the perception of how other African Americans might view the justice.

The news and social media also play a role in framing issues that elicit a response. Research results in psychology and political science suggest that media organizations are effective in reinforcing predisposed attitudes about certain policies and issues.[63] Individuals will watch news outlets or participate in social media platforms (e.g., Facebook, Twitter, YouTube) that reinforce what they already believe or that coincide with existing predisposed attitudes.[64] As Cohen suggested 55 years ago, the news media do not directly tell people what to think, but they are effective in telling people what to think about.[65] Furthermore, depending on the news outlet or social media platform, policies and or issues are framed as negative or positive on society. Divergent framing on an issue particularly in politics can lead to sociopolitical conflicts resulting in an "us versus them" culture.

As such, microaggressions are framed in a multitude of ways. The most common framing of microaggressions occurs when an individual or group wants to convey superiority over an individual or group they feel is inferior. This microaggressive approach has been used throughout American history, and this method continues to be used today. Consider the physical elimination and removal of Native Americans and the characterization of Native Americans as "merciless savages"[66] in the Declaration of Independence. Speeches by America's Founding Fathers purposely excluded and denigrated slaves; political policies such as the Chinese Exclusion Act of 1882, Japanese internment camps in the 1940s, Operation Wetback in the 1950s, and the 2017 Muslim ban as well as numerous other policies purposely meant to frame individuals and groups as inferior or un-American.

## Partisan Sorting and Polarization

Social group connections and/or membership in a group have a lasting effect on individuals. When a person feels they belong to a group, their actions and reactions typically align with the rest of the group. Keeping this in mind, research continues to show that when individuals feel emotionally connected to a political party, they are more likely to identify with the party; and when an individual feels their party is threatened, they react to the situation.[67] Their reaction is based on a social and emotional connection they feel as part of the group. Even when an individual may have an opposing opinion about an issue, their emotional connection to the group (i.e., political party) overrides other factors, resulting in the individual defending the group (i.e., political party). More significant, belonging to a group has been found to cause people to hold biased views against other groups.[68] Taken as a whole, people will self-sort into groups with similar interests and identities and will protect the group.

In this context, social group membership and how people act and react to political microaggressions is important to consider. In political science, partisan sorting occurs when individuals (i.e., voters) sort themselves into the different parties based on the cues provided by the political parties. Typically, U.S. individuals will sort into the two main parties, Democratic or Republican, which influence behavior. Cues provide shortcuts that help voters interpret political issues that may be complex, and they help sort voters along party lines.[69] For example, in the 2016 U.S. presidential election, the mantra of "Build the Wall" provided the cue that one of the candidates was going to be strict on immigration. This cue provided limited information, but it was enough so that voters either supported or opposed the political party. Partisan sorting based on cues is typically learned early in life through family socialization and remains stable over time.[70]

Although not the subject of this research, partisan sorting may play a role in how people respond or react to political microaggressions. Recall from above, when people are part of a group they have a social and emotional connection to the group, including political parties. If one party is the recipient of a political microaggression from the opposing party, individuals of the recipient party will come to the defense of their party. However, if an individual is part of the perpetrator party, their response to the microaggression may be different. Because individuals have an emotional connection to one of the major political parties, a political microaggression may seem to be either a threat or warranted. When elected officials engage in political microaggressions, individuals who identify with the party will have a favorable view of the official and their use of a political microaggression. This in turn can provide a platform for regular citizens to engage in the use of microaggressions against individuals they perceive as nonmembers of their group. A case in point would be the Lou Holtz vignette at the beginning of this chapter, which creates an "us versus them" sociopolitical environment.

## Polarization

When microaggressions are framed as an "us versus them" phenomenon, economic, political, and social polarization begins to take place. *Polarization* is a divergence in attitudes and beliefs in politics, religion, education, immigration, affirmative action, the death penalty, and a host of other issues. Polarization occurs when an individual or group begins framing economic, political, and social issues in a manner that resonates with individuals or groups. Framing can be constructive or ideologically extreme, depending on an individual's policy preferences. Polarization results in individuals self-sorting and aligning with either the constructive or the ideologically extreme viewpoint. Because of how an issue is framed, polarization affects how individuals respond to a particular issue. Take for example the Lou Holtz vignette at the beginning of this chapter. Holtz states that immigrants are an "invasion" to the United States and should learn to speak English and "become us." If an individual is a supporter of stricter immigration policies, they will align and self-sort with Holtz. However, other individuals may find his comments off-putting and would prefer to self-sort out of extremist views.

An interesting thing starts to happen when demographics begin to change. Framing and polarization begin to increase, exacerbating the "us versus them" phenomenon. Nowhere is this more acute than in political rhetoric. Political elites will use microaggressions to frame individuals, groups, and organizations in a manner that creates a polarizing society. Fifty years ago, Hubert Blalock, in his seminal book *Toward a Theory of Minority Group Relations*, suggested that a large minority presence living in close proximity to whites would provoke economic and political threats among whites, resulting in prejudicial attitudes. Dominant groups react to the competition for limited resources and the perceived threat from inferior or subordinate groups.[71] Political rhetoric infused with microaggressions taps into these fears, creating a polarized environment among groups. This is especially significant as demographics have begun to change, and groups that once held the majority are in jeopardy of losing or at least having to share the economic, political, and social control that they have had since the founding of the United States.

## Conclusion

This chapter introduced the reader to microaggressions and its various forms. While we have all likely been perpetrators of microaggressions, we have not all been victims of microaggressions. This chapter established that the use of microaggressions is not a new phenomenon in education, employment, and politics. What is new is the format in which microaggressions are communicated. In a technological era where cable television, social media, and the Internet are accessible 24/7, an avenue has been created in which perpetrators of microaggressions are free to espouse their comments with little oversight. While some may argue that individuals have become too politically correct or sensitive, the fact remains that using microaggressions is a way to belittle and insult others. From framing an individual as a "snowflake" to the use of a racial slur, the damage inflicted from unabated microaggressions is lasting, which can create a long-lasting polarizing environment. Political rhetoric matters in U.S. politics because rhetoric can be used as a weapon to create an environment where elected officials and regular citizens have no regrets in snubbing and discriminating against certain individuals and groups.

# CHAPTER TWO

# Changing Demographics: From Minority to Majority

Amado Morales, 64, of Floydada, Texas, got involved in local politics 36 years ago after serving in the U.S. Army. Morales was elected in 2017 to the Commissioners Court Precinct 4 in Floyd County. He is the only Latino member of the court in a county with a 53 percent Latino population. Prior to serving as a county commissioner, in the 1980s Morales was elected to the Floydada City Council. Morales' initial election to the City Council was met with hostility by [white] cotton processors who had regularly conducted business with him but were now threatened by his election. Morales recalls, "I had hauled cotton for gins for years, but one day they said, 'We don't need you anymore. We'll lose our customers, our growers. You're the problem, trying to stir up shit around here.'" They told me, "We need to get rid of this guy. We need to cut this twig right out. Because if it grows it's gonna be a trunk and we won't be able to deal with it. We have to make him suffer. Squeeze him out of Floyd County." In a small conservative Texas town and county, Morales puts politics into perspective: "They don't want to share power, it's their way of life."[1]

As the vignette above suggests, demographics began to shift in this small Texas town as early as the 1980s. The election of a Latino to the City Council in Floydada, Texas, was met with anger and hostility by some whites. To put the election of Amado Morales into perspective, census data indicates that in 1980 individuals identifying as "Spanish" (the term used in the 1980 Census) accounted for 34 percent of the population, and individuals identifying as African American accounted for 6 percent of the population.[2] At the time, minorities accounted for less than half of the overall population in Floydada, Texas. What is significant about this vignette is the reaction by the community: one member of the cotton industry that Morales had known for years stated, "You're the problem, trying to stir up shit around here," and another community acquaintance reacted to the election of Morales with "We need to cut this twig right out. Because if it grows it's gonna be a trunk and we won't be able to deal with it. We have to make him suffer. Squeeze him out of Floyd County." Why would some members of the community respond in this manner to a military veteran elected to a local city council? This chapter explores how demographics have begun to shift and how majority populations may be in jeopardy of potentially losing the political, economic, and social control they have had since the nation's founding. As illustrated from Morales's recollection, some community members may not be enthusiastic about the implications of shifting demographics. Not that all citizens in a community will respond negatively, but it is safe to say that the social constructs of race have historically been a factor—a negative factor. This point becomes more poignant when we consider the possible shift to a majority-minority population, where the plurality is minority. This shift may cause some consternation among individuals soon to be the new minority population.

Recall from Chapter 1 that microassaults are direct, intentional, verbal, and divisive comments that communicate hostile, derogatory, or negative insults toward a person, group, or organization. Elected officials at all levels of government engage in negative political rhetoric to deliberately exclude a person, group, or organization, while at the same time providing sound bites to rally supporters. Microaggressions matter in U.S. politics because this type of rhetoric marginalizes individuals and groups, conveying a message that these groups are less desirable and that it is acceptable for members of society to perceive them negatively. Furthermore, unlike the traditional view that most microaggressions are ingenuous, this research contends that political microaggressions are intentional and calculated.

Analogous to political microaggressions are microassaults, a variation of microaggressions that can manifest as "old-fashioned racism" where an action is conscious, deliberate, and considered an intentionally biased attitude; expressed by a violent verbal or nonverbal attack meant to hurt a marginalized person or group; and can be characterized by name calling, persistent discriminatory actions, and avoidant behavior.[3] In the vignette above, Morales was the recipient of deliberate verbal attacks and avoidant behavior meant to denigrate him and his election to the Floydada City Council. In the end, Morales won his bid for city council and was elected, indicating that some community members did support his candidacy. But the implications of those who did not support Morales tend to be problematic as demographics begin to shift.

## Breaking Down the Numbers: Demographic Shifts

As of 2016, the annual estimate of the resident population in the United States reached 325 million,[4] and by 2050 population projections are estimated to reach 400 million.[5] Minority groups such as African Americans, Asian Americans, and Latinos currently comprise a larger share of the U.S. population when compared to any other period in history. The demographics of the population is more ethnically and racially diverse, resulting in the United States becoming more multicultural and multilingual. Although ethnic and racial diversification continues to grow, as of 2014, non-Hispanic whites still accounted for the largest share of the population at slightly over 50 percent.[6] However, population projections indicate that by 2060, the share of non-Hispanic whites will fall to less than 50 percent of the overall U.S. population.[7] As illustrated in Tables 2.1 and 2.2, 2000 and 2010 census data and 2016 American Community Survey data indicate that states such as Arizona, Georgia, Maryland, and New York have minority populations that constitute over 40 percent of the state's population, while states such as California, Hawaii, New Mexico, and Texas all have minority populations that exceed 50 percent of the total state population.[8] Demographics have begun to shift, and the majority non-Hispanic white population may be at risk of losing the political control they have had for centuries.[9] Changing demographics and the perceived threat of a minority "takeover" creates conditions where microaggressive behavior and polarization begin to manifest in political discourse, policies, and actions. The continued growth in minority and multiracial populations challenges the narrow Eurocentric framing about government, elected officials, and democracy. Changing demographics raise questions as to what group(s) get(s) a seat at the table in discussing political and social issues that affect all Americans.

Some of the shift in changing demographics is attributed to the continued immigration of Asian and Latino populations. For example, between 2000 and 2010, the Asian population increased faster than any other racial or ethnic group in the United States.[10] The Asian population increased four times faster than the total U.S. population: the total U.S. population increased by 9.7 percent, from 281.4 million in 2000 to 308.7 million in 2010; the Asian population increased by 43 percent from 10.2 million to 14.7 million during the same period.[11] Similarly, the Latino population increased four times faster than the total U.S. population between 2000 and 2010: from 15.2 million to over 27.3 million, an increase of 43 percent.[12] During this same period, the African American population grew at a slower rate when compared to Asian and Latino populations, increasing by 15 percent to over 38.9 million of the total U.S. population.[13] The data indicates that not only did single minority populations increase between 2000 and 2010, but there was also an increase

Table 2.1    Change in U.S. Minority Population by Top 10 States: 2000
and 2010

| State | 2000 Percent Minority | 2010 Percent Minority | Percentage Change |
|---|---|---|---|
| Arizona | 36.2 | 42.2 | 16.57 |
| California | 53.3 | 59.9 | 12.38 |
| Georgia | 37.4 | 44.1 | 17.91 |
| Hawaii | 77.1 | 77.3 | .25 |
| Louisiana | 37.5 | 39.7 | 5.86 |
| Maryland | 37.9 | 45.3 | 19.52 |
| Mississippi | 39.3 | 42 | 6.87 |
| New Mexico | 55.3 | 59.5 | 7.59 |
| New York | 38 | 41.7 | 9.73 |
| Texas | 47.6 | 54.7 | 14.91 |

*Source:* Karen R. Humes, Nicolas A. Jones, and Roberto R. Ramirez, *Overview of Race and Hispanic Origin: 2010* (Washington DC: U.S. Census Bureau, 2011), https://www.census.gov/prod/cen2010/briefs/c2010br-02.pdf.

Table 2.2    Change in U.S. Minority Population by Top 10 States: 2000–
2010 and 2010–2017

| State | 2000–2010 Percent Change | 2010–2017 Percent Change |
|---|---|---|
| Arizona | 16.57 | 3.91 |
| California | 12.38 | 2.87 |
| Georgia | 17.91 | 4.04 |
| Hawaii | .25 | .43 |
| Louisiana | 5.86 | 2.54 |
| Maryland | 19.52 | 4.88 |
| Mississippi | 6.87 | 1.88 |
| New Mexico | 7.59 | 3.06 |
| New York | 9.73 | 4.53 |
| Texas | 14.91 | 3.44 |

*Source:* Karen R. Humes, Nicolas A. Jones, and Roberto R. Ramirez, *Overview of Race and Hispanic Origin: 2010* (Washington DC: U.S. Census Bureau, 2011), https://www.census.gov/prod/cen2010/briefs/c2010br-02.pdf.; U.S. Census Bureau, American Community Survey, Characteristics of Native and Foreign Born Populations 5-Year Estimates, https://factfinder.census.gov/bkmk/table/1.0/en/ACS/16_5YR/S0501/0100000US%7C04 00000US27%7C0400000US27.05000.

in multiracial identification. For example, the total number of African Americans reporting one or more races increased by 1 percent, or 3.1 million. Similarly, in the Latino community, 6 percent or 3 million Latinos identified as multiracial.

Figures 2.1 and 2.2 illustrate the disparity in minority population changes by region when compared to the non-Hispanic white-alone population. All four regions experienced large minority population growth, with the South and West regions experiencing the largest increases. Southern states have traditionally been home to large numbers of African Americans, but trends indicate that states such as Georgia, Louisiana, and Mississippi now have a Latino population that comprises 40 percent of the total state population. However, the 2016 American Community Survey data seems to indicate that six years after the 2010 Census, the growing number of minorities in the South began to slow. With the upcoming 2020 Census we will be able to examine the full extent of minority population growth or deceleration. Figure 2.3 illustrates the minimal growth of the non-Hispanic white-alone population from 2000, 2010, and 2016. The graph indicates that between 2000 and 2010 the non-Hispanic white-alone population decreased in the Northwest by 3.4 percent, and the Midwest experienced a 0.6 percent decline. The South and the West both experienced growth at 4.21 percent and 3 percent, but when compared to the growth in minority populations, the non-Hispanic white-alone growth was flat or nominal at the very most (Figures 2.1 and 2.2).

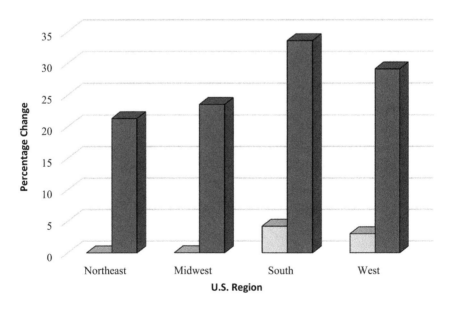

**Figure 2.1**  Population Percentage Change 2000 to 2010

*Source:* U.S. Census Bureau, Overview of Race and Hispanic Origin: 2010

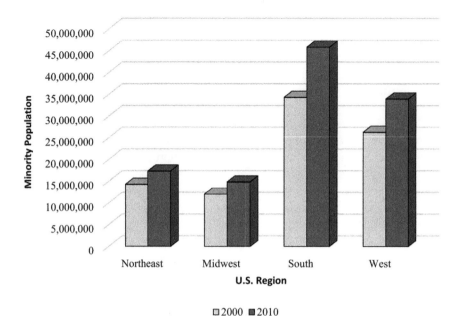

**Figure 2.2** Minority Population by U.S. Region: Comparison 2000 and 2010

*Source:* U.S. Census Bureau, Overview of Race and Hispanic Origin: 2010

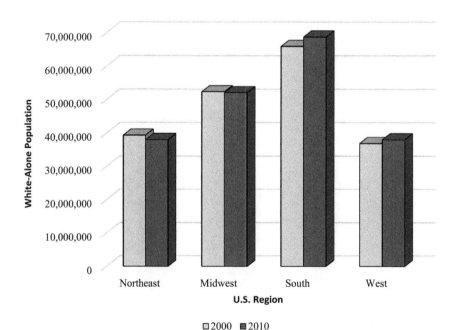

**Figure 2.3** Non-Hispanic White Alone by U.S. Region: Comparison 2000 and 2010

*Source:* U.S. Census Bureau, Overview of Race and Hispanic Origin: 2010

In addition, for non-Hispanic whites the changing ethnic composition is further exacerbated by an increase in undocumented immigrants. Data shows that at least half of the estimated 11–12 million undocumented immigrants in the United States originate from Mexico or Central and Latin American countries.[14] The rapid ethnic proliferation in the United States has the potential of changing communities, political institutions, and public policies. As a result, and to a degree, non-Hispanic whites are attuned to the changing ethnic balance and political environment precipitated by the growth in Latino and undocumented populations.[15] The continued and visible growth of Latino and undocumented immigrants affects public policy at all levels of government. In a stagnant economy, undocumented immigrants may negatively affect already constrained public budgets. In a growing economy, undocumented populations may supplement state and local coffers through contributions to tax structures.[16] As Stephen Legomsky emphasized in his analysis of immigrants and the justice system, nativist impulses have a number of origins within a community; there is economic uncertainty, fear of the growing numbers of immigrants, a possible increase in crime, overt racism toward certain groups, or simply anger toward the federal government and its ineptness regarding immigration.[17] For some native-born citizens, the growing number of Latinos and undocumented immigrants inflames a sense of nativism, which leads to defensive posturing. The natural inclination for some groups becomes protecting communities against these growing ethnic groups that they see as threatening American mores and values.

## Why Does It Matter?

So far, in this chapter, the reader has been introduced to data that indicates demographics are changing in the United States. Some readers may be thinking, "Why does this matter?" and "How does this relate to political rhetoric and microaggressions?" Changing demographics matter because, historically, political rhetoric and microaggressions have been used to frame certain groups as inferior or not "American enough" in order to suppress economic, political, and social opportunities for minority groups (see the Amado Morales vignette at the beginning of this chapter and Chapter 4 on a discussion regarding slavery, the Chinese Exclusion Act, and other government suppressive acts). Microaggressions in U.S. politics matter because this rhetoric is effective at creating an atmosphere where politicians and ordinary American citizens feel indifferent about espousing hostile rhetoric against certain individuals and groups. Ironically, this rhetoric results in discriminatory public policies that effect 99 percent of the population, which includes microaggression perpetrators. In addition, shifting demographics matter because these changes impact languages spoken, customary cultures, religious observations, and how groups view and interact with each other—not all of which will be met openly and enthusiastically.

Recall from Chapter 1 that framing suggests how issues should be examined and how they should be dealt with if needed.[18] Take for example, in the year 2017, how some ordinary citizens frame political parties. Americans Against the Republican Party and the Anti-Republican Crusaders are Facebook communities that portray members of the Republican Party as only concerned with wealth, as frauds, and as destructive leaders. On the other side are Facebook communities such as Americans Against the Democratic Party who frame Democrats as idiots, crybabies, and sore losers. Framing provides a guide for how an opinion should be formed about an issue or group; it allows the disseminator of information to impress upon followers (friends, family members, coworkers, acquaintances) how a topic or group should be viewed.[19]

Consider how Donald Trump, the 2016 Republican presidential candidate, characterized individuals from Mexico. Trump framed all immigrants from Mexico as undocumented, rapists, drug dealers, and killers.[20] Verbal comments and online postings that generalize an entire population or group create a polarizing environment, which breeds dissension resulting in divisions and anger toward the minority group. Now, consider the perceived threat of a minority economic, political, and social "takeover." Next, insert "people from Mexico" into the frame; the result is that some ordinary citizens will want to preserve their dominance over economic, political, and social arenas, which are being infringed upon by Mexicans as framed by verbal comments and online postings. These arenas become avenues for negative political rhetoric and microaggressive behavior, and polarization begins to take place in political discourse, policies, and actions. More important, framing provides the cues that result in hostile rhetoric and microaggressive behavior. The use of microaggressions matter—they are not isolated to the highest political office but rather are rampant at all levels of government and in society. Hostile rhetoric matters because it creates conditions where ordinary American citizens such as family, friends, neighbors, and members of a church feel comfortable disparaging and stereotyping certain groups and individuals.

## The Political Impact of Growing Minority Groups

One of the key issues political elites are struggling to respond to is the growing number of minorities and their demand to participate in the democratic process. Since the conceptualization of government institutions in the United States by white, Anglo-Saxon, Protestant men, no other racial or ethnic group has come close to holding absolute economic, political, and social power as designed by the Founding Fathers. Howard Zinn points out that the Founding Fathers intentionally created a document (the U.S. Constitution) deliberately excluding black people and Native Americans to maintain their superiority:

> The inferior positions of blacks, the exclusion of Indians from the new society, the establishment of supremacy for the rich and powerful in the new nation—all this was already settled in the colonies by the time of the Revolution. With England out of the way, it could now be put on paper, solidified, regularized, made legitimate, by the Constitution of the United States, drafted at a convention of Revolutionary leaders in Philadelphia.[21]

Similarly, Charles Beard, in *An Economic Interpretation of the Constitution of the United States*, points out that the Constitution was specifically written to maintain a certain structure in American society, excluding from power

> the slaves, the indentured servants, the mass of men who could not qualify for voting under the property tests imposed by the state constitutions and laws, and women, disfranchised and subjected to the discriminations of the common law. These groups were, therefore, not represented in the Convention which drafted the Constitution, except under the theory that representation has no relation to voting.[22]

Simply stated, Beard maintains that the Founders who supported the Constitution did so on the basis of how the "Document" could benefit them economically, and "the leaders who supported the Constitution in the ratifying conventions represented the same economic groups as the members of the Philadelphia Convention."[23] The U.S. political system, along with the founding documents that shape policies, was drafted and adopted to maintain a slave economy.[24] Moreover, institutional structures such as the legal system, housing markets, education, and employment sectors have also been used to limit some individuals' ability to act politically and economically.[25] This is why changing demographics matters, because the United States was founded on documents and institutions that continue to exclude numerous groups from the democratic process. While this may seem extreme, it is important to understand the historical process of how one group through founding documents and institutions has continued to hold unquestioned economic, political, and social power.

The response to changing demographics can be multifaceted. Research examining the effects of increases in Latinos and undocumented immigrants suggests that an increase in diversity triggers conservative ideological attitudes among native-born citizens.[26] Part of the anxiety toward Latinos[27] and immigrants[28] emanates from the groups themselves and how these groups are perceived.[29] Perceptions toward these out-groups range from low-skill, low-wage workers to unassimilating populations with high fertility rates.[30] Negative perceptions are further magnified when these groups seem to be tipping the ethnic balance away from an "American" identity.

Political elites will use negative perceptions to limit minorities' entry into the democratic process[31] through nativist rhetoric that questions if a minority group is "American enough" to be emblematic of white, Anglo-Saxon elite norms. This framing sets the stage in which some minorities are seen as not assimilating to the dominant culture. *Assimilation* is the process in which an individual or group culture begins to resemble those of the dominant group.[32] Assimilation concerns are usually reserved for castigating immigrants as non-conformists. Framing some minority groups as lacking assimilation creates a negative hierarchical view of the minority group. In essence, the group that is negatively categorized will find themselves at the bottom of the economic, political, and social hierarchy regardless of their contributions to society.

An alternative response to shifting demographics is stereotyping minority groups as inferior based on their religion, education, or socioeconomic status and by discriminating against minorities through the enactment of stringent policies such as voting laws that disenfranchise people of color.[33] Although the future might sound bleak for some minority groups, we must be careful not to frame all white, Anglo-Saxon political elites as autocratic, self-interested individuals. Numerous Anglo political elites can and do support an inclusive institutional democracy that recognizes the diversification of the political landscape.

An important although more difficult response would be for minority groups to increase their presence in the political arena by becoming more active in the democratic process. Historically, minorities have low voter turnout percentages when compared to non-Hispanic whites. African Americans vote in higher numbers when compared to Latinos and Asians; in turn, Latinos at times vote at higher rates than Asians and vice versa.[34] For example, in the 2016 U.S. presidential election, African Americans were 12 percent of the total vote, Latinos 11 percent, and Asians 4 percent;[35] these results are similar to turnout rates in the 2012 presidential elections where African Americans were 13 percent of the total vote, Latinos 10 percent, and Asians 3 percent.[36] Although the continued immigration of Latino and Asian populations is a major reason for changing demographics, these groups are not monolithic in their political behavior. Unlike African American voters who tend to unite and coalesce around certain candidates and vote at a higher percentage,[37] Latino and Asian voters are still on the periphery of having a significant political impact. The 2012 U.S. presidential election of Barack Obama did indicate that as a whole Latinos can make a difference in elections when they vote. Data indicates that 75 percent of Latinos who went to the polls voted for Obama, which was the highest percentage support any presidential candidate had received from Latinos.[38]

## Challenges in Shifting to a Majority-Minority Population

Ethnic minorities of various national origins are typically considered monolithic groups[39] who share the same interests. But as Nicolás Vaca chronicles in *The Presumed Alliance*, Latinos and African Americans have divergent political and social interests that lead to conflicts over power and resources. Vaca details how Latinos and African Americans view each other and the hostility that occurs as a result of a growing Latino population—changing demographics. As part of his analysis, Vaca introduces the reader to the *Charlotte Post*, an African American newspaper, which interviewed African American residents in Charlotte, North Carolina, shortly after the 2000 Census released its data indicating that the Latino population was almost equivalent in numbers to that of African Americans.[40] In one of the interviews, an African American computer technician made the following comments about the growing Latino population:

> I definitely think they are people to fear. . . . They travel in packs. They like to play stupid acting as if they don't understand English when you know they do. A group of them will sit around and talk to each other in their language. They could be plotting to kill you and you would never know it. They are taking over. They're taking all our jobs. Slowly but surely. I just don't care to be around them. They make my skin crawl, I keep my ideas to myself. This might sound bad, but I don't go around making remarks about them to other people. So, only God can judge me.[41]

Another African American computer engineer expressed his views on changing demographics in the following way: "I'm not surprised that Latinos are nearly even with Blacks. Hispanics come over here, start businesses, and multiply like rabbits. . . . It's no surprise they outnumber us because they have a baby every year."[42] From these accounts, there is an obvious conflict in how various minority groups view and interact with each other. Microassaults and microinvalidations are not reserved for majority group interactions; they are also used within minority groups as they struggle for resources and power.

Today as in the past, preconceived stereotypes and biases are often the source of interethnic conflict between minority groups. Minority groups that do not reject the use of political microaggressions by elected officials and candidates and instead support stereotypic views about other minority groups inadvertently allow the majority group to retain their position at the top of the hierarchy. Recall, unlike prior research on microaggressions, this study maintains that microaggressions are intentional and not unconscious acts. At the macro level, institutions controlled by the majority consistently sustain racial subordination and inequalities.[43] Thus, African Americans and Latinos who engage in microaggressions against each other create auspicious conditions for polarization between the groups. Polarization and divisiveness among minority groups allow the majority group to retain control. Historically, the racial hierarchy created by the majority ruling class has provided economic, political, and social benefits for that group.[44] In an illustration of how the majority group has the potential of retaining political, economic, and social control, take the account from an interview between Representative Steve King (R-IA) and Iowa radio host Jan Mickelson. King and Mickelson spoke about changing demographics in response to Univision's Jorge Ramos's comment that in the near future whites would become the majority-minority group in the United States:

> Host: Is there anything about your tweets over the weekend that you would change?
>
> King: Not at all, Jan. I'll probably be putting some more out here that calls them to think a little bit more.
>
> King: Their effort here is to be celebrating because the United States is moving towards becoming, the whites becoming a minority, a majority-minority within the country according to what their plan is.
>
> Host: Now, if you talk that way they would label you a racist.
>
> King: Yes, that's true. That's true. But what are they after? What is their utopia? They're dividing people. They're pitting people against each other. And Jorge Ramos's stock in trade is identifying and trying to drive wedges between race.
>
> King: Race and ethnicity, I should say to be more correct. When you start accentuating the difference, then you start ending up with people that are at each other's throats. And he's adding up Hispanics and blacks into what he predicts will be in greater number than whites in America. I will predict that Hispanics and the blacks will be fighting each other before that happens.[45]

On the surface, King seems to be saying all the right things about an inclusive environment and the problem of accentuating differences between groups. However, King has a long-documented history of microaggressions. King's comments in his interview are clear examples of microinsults and microinvalidations toward African Americans and Latinos. Recall that a microinsult is often unconscious behavior or a verbal remark that is disguised as a compliment or positive statement directed toward an individual or group. And a microinvalidation negates or nullifies the viewpoints of people of color. Recall from Chapter 1 that political microaggressions are direct, intentional, verbal, and divisive comments that communicate hostile, derogatory, or negative insults toward a person, group, or organization. And, in contrast to the idea that microaggressions are often innocent and uncon-sciousness, this research argues that microaggressions are intentional and purposeful and provide perpetrators an avenue for expressing internalized biases. In the King interview, he purposely expresses his bias by predicting that Hispanics and African Americans will be fighting each other before a majority-minority shift happens. These comments are not unlike what Vaca found in his analysis; the difference, however, is in the messenger and how changing demographics are framed. King's comments come after his tweet that American civilization cannot be restored with somebody else's babies (this was tweeted in reference to continued immigration in the United States). King defended his tweet by stating that his comments were not about race, a classic example of color-blind racism.[46] King's comments are jarring and communicate divisive and hostile insults toward specific groups, which equate to political microaggressions.

Another method in which political microaggressions exacerbate the fram-ing of "us versus them," making it difficult to transition to a majority-minority population, is through the continued reinforcement of microassaults or "old-fashioned racism." During the 2016 U.S. presidential election, Repub-lican candidate Donald Trump made numerous verbal and online comments regarding Latinos. In one instance, at a Trump campaign rally, anti-Trump protestors gathered at the event. The next morning, Trump tweeted: "Many of the thugs that attacked the peaceful Trump supporters in San Jose were illegals. They burned the American flag and laughed at police."[47] To Trump it was inconceivable that Latino anti-Trump protestors could be U.S. citizens denouncing his anti-immigrant rhetoric in the campaign. Instead, with one tweet, the microassault was that all protestors were undocumented. In another instance, on Cinco de Mayo, a celebration of Mexican culture and heritage, Trump tweeted a picture of himself eating Mexican food. The tweet read "Happy #CincoDeMayo! The best taco bowls are made in Trump Tower Grill. I love Hispanics!"[48] In this tweet, the microinvalidation is the assump-tion that all Hispanics are monolithic and from Mexican descent. Again, an example of color-blind racism and political microaggression. Trump gen-eralizes about the Latinos at the campaign rally, "they were all illegal," which was a direct, intentional, verbal, divisive online comment that communicated hostile, derogatory, or negative insults toward a group. Trump engaged in negative political rhetoric to rally supporters while at the same time delib-erately blacklisting a group. Political microaggressions target minorities and marginalize groups, conveying the message that these groups are less desirable and that it is appropriate for members of society to perceive them negatively.

Latinos are not the only minority group Trump has microaggressed. Trump was the leading instigator of the birtherism conspiracy theory levied against the first African American president of the United States, Barack

Obama. Trump argued that Obama was not born in the United States and thus was not a U.S. citizen—as such, he could not be a legitimate U.S. president. However, Obama was born in Hawaii to an American mother from Kansas, while his father was from Kenya. Two forms of microaggressions are at play with the birther movement from a political elite. The first is a micro-assault or old-fashioned racism. Creating a false narrative and framing it so that the first African American president of the United States is seen as illegitimately holding the office of the presidency cannot be understated.[49] While Trump's internal motivations for initiating a falsehood is outside the purview of this research, what we do know is that Trump has not accused other presidents of illegitimately holding the office. Second, Trump's rhetoric is problematic because he was successful in creating a false narrative, a microinvalidation negating and nullifying the existence of the first African American president. For this type of systematic political microaggression to persist requires institutional and organizational support to fan the flames of racism and polarization.

The racist system categorizes and divides human beings from each other and severely impedes the development of a common consciousness. It fractures human nature by separating those socially defined as the "superior race" against those defined as the "inferior race."[50] Institutional and organizational resistance will be challenges minority groups will face as they transition to a majority-minority population. Changing demographics is a significant issue because historically the majority has used political microaggressions to frame minority groups as inferior or not "American" in order to control economic, political, and social opportunities for minority groups. A growing minority population will impact how political elites respond to changing demographics, not all of which will be met receptively.[51] Political microaggressions are intentional and purposeful and are used by perpetrators to express their internalized biases.

## Difficulty Overcoming Perceptions of Race and Microaggressions

Changes in race and ethnicity can have important implications for institutions and systems. At stake is the continuation of a smooth operational economic, political, and social system. The dynamics of a changing racial environment are far reaching. Changes create perceptions, and perceptions create action and opportunities. Perceptions about certain groups can be accurate or inaccurate, and actions and opportunities can be negative or positive. All of which will exacerbate the fear that institutions and systems will change because of a racial hierarchical realignment. Add to that divisive political rhetoric infused with microaggressions targeting minority groups, and the fear creates negative actions. Recall from Chapter 1 how rhetoric from the 2016 U.S. presidential campaign led to negative actions: Adam W. Purinton shot and killed Srinivas Kuchibhotla, a legal immigrant from India, and the incident at a West Texas WalMart between a native Pakistani physician and a white man. In both cases, the perpetrators shouted racial slurs and "Get out of my country" and "Make America great again," slogans used by the Republican candidate. The perception that immigrants are "invading and taking over America" resulted in these two men acting out their biases—more significant, during their attacks they used combative racial slurs that included micro-aggressions used by one of the candidates.

One of the difficulties in discussing changing demographics is acknowledging that political elites and the media influence and frame the perceptions people have about each other and how one group impacts the other. When political microaggressions are used as divisive tools to win an election or garner support for a candidate, an inaccurate perception about a group can be difficult to overcome. When certain minority groups are framed as lazy, undocumented, unambitious, or abusers of services provided by institutions and systems, a change to a majority-minority population will be problematic for some individuals in the majority.[52] The difficulty stems from the perceptions groups have about each other and the self-sorting (polarization) that occurs when certain groups are considered inferior.[53]

As an illustration of how diverse groups view each other, a Gallup poll found that different racial groups see the treatment of other racial groups from diametrically opposed perspectives. In a 2016 poll, survey participants were asked how they felt various groups in society were treated, specifically how blacks were treated. Fifty-six percent of white respondents were very satisfied to somewhat satisfied in how blacks were treated in society. Black and Latino respondents had a different view of race relations: only 32 percent of blacks and 47 percent of Latinos were very satisfied to somewhat satisfied in how blacks were treated in society. In the same poll, survey participants were asked how they felt Hispanics were treated in society. Similar to the African American results, 59 percent of white respondents were very satisfied to somewhat satisfied in how Hispanics were treated in society. Compare this to black and Hispanic respondents, who viewed the treatment of Hispanics in society as 43 percent and 46 percent very satisfied to somewhat satisfied.[54] In both these cases, almost 60 percent of white respondents perceived the treatment of blacks and Hispanics as satisfactory. However, individuals who identified as black or Hispanic had a different perspective on how they thought they were treated in society. Only approximately 30 to 40 percent of black and Hispanic respondents were satisfied in how they were treated, a difference of 30 and 20 percent from white respondents respectively. The spatial difference in perceptions is sizable—that is, whites perceive the treatment of minorities as satisfactory, while minorities see their treatment as less than satisfactory.

Let us briefly consider the work of Joe Feagin, who conducts extensive research on societal racism and the issues of inequality. Feagin writes that the framing of issues by whites is very influential. In this case, the perceptions that whites have about the treatment of minority groups as satisfactory in society allows whites to continue to dominate economic, political, and social environments:

> In North America and elsewhere a dominant, white-created racial frame
> . . . provides an overarching and generally destructive worldview, one that
> extends across divisions of class, gender, and age. Since its full develop
> ment over the course of the seventeenth century, this powerful frame has
> provided the vantage point from which most whites have constantly
> viewed North American society. Its centrality in white minds is what
> makes it a dominant frame throughout the country and, indeed, the West
> ern world. Over time, this powerful frame has been elaborated by, and
> imposed on, the minds of most Americans, becoming thereby the coun
> try's dominant "frame of mind" and "frame of reference" in regard to racial
> matters.[55]

A white-created racial frame will be a challenge for minority groups to overcome as demographics continue to change and as political microaggressions increase and are disseminated relatively seamlessly through social media avenues such as Twitter, Facebook, Periscope, and many others. The transition to majority-minority will be met with institutional and systematic changes in order to retain the racial hierarchical advantage regardless of whether the hierarchy realigns.

In another example of how race perceptions lead to polarization, the same Gallup poll also asked participants what role the government should have in improving the social and economic positions of blacks and other minority groups.[56] The results are revealing in that the visual prism in which citizens view each other is contextual, and not all groups view each other or the issues pertinent to that group equally. For example, 28 percent of whites indicated that the government should play a major role in improving social and economic positions of blacks and other minority groups, while 46 percent of whites indicated the government should have a minor role. Contrast those findings with the responses from blacks and Hispanics; 64 percent of blacks and 63 percent of Hispanics indicated that the government should play a major role in improving social and economic positions for these groups. A whole host of issues can be attributed to the difference in perspectives about the role of government in improving social and economic positions for minorities. For example, underrepresentation, housing discrimination, voter disenfranchisement, economic inequality, and access to higher education directly affect communities of color. However, as a matter of perception, whites see minorities as "moving to the front of the line" ahead of whites,[57] thus there is no need to have government involvement in improving their social and economic position. Since the perception and framing are one in which demographics are changing and giving minority groups a perceived edge, the majority group will oppose institutional changes that benefit minorities.[58] Instead institutional changes that hinder the progress of minority groups will be instituted as a way for the majority to retain control.

On August 2, 2017, the National Association for the Advancement of Colored People (NAACP) issued a travel advisory for African Americans to use extreme caution when traveling throughout the state of Missouri.[59] This was the first time the NAACP issued a travel advisory warning for an entire U.S. state. The travel advisory was in response to "questionable race-based incidents occurring statewide"[60] and the signing of Senate Bill 43 (SB43) by Republican governor Eric Greitens with support from the University of Missouri System and other groups. The NAACP issued the travel advisory due to recent African American deaths, harassment, and the state attorney general's report that found African American motorists were stopped at a rate of 75 percent higher than whites.[61] What is striking about the attorney general's report is that African Americans only comprised 10.9 percent of the Missouri population yet were stopped at a much higher rate compared to whites who accounted for 82.76 percent of the population.[62] Additionally, Missouri's SB43 makes it more difficult for victims of religious, gender, or racial discrimination to seek damages—victims have a higher legal standard to prove that discrimination occurred. The racial profiling of African Americans is a microassault, and SB43 has the potential of being a microinvalidation nullifying religious, gender, and racial bias. Similarly, in May 2017, the American Civil Liberties Union issued a travel alert for individuals traveling in and to Texas. The travel alert was in response to Senate Bill 4 (SB4), also termed the "sanctuary cities" law, which allows police officers in the state to confirm a person's immigration status during a routine traffic stop—based on racial profiling if the citizen is presumed to be foreign.[63] In addition, SB 4 prohibits cities from providing sanctuary for undocumented immigrants and requires all local law enforcement officers to liaise with federal immigration authorities. Superficially, SB4 may seem to be a deterrent for undocumented immigration; however, Texas has a long Latino history, and it places individuals of Latino descent at risk of arbitrarily being stopped and questioned about their immigration status based on phenotypic characteristics. SB4 could function as a microassault policy that racially profiles Latinos and foreigners based on a perceived threat from a growing immigrant group. These types of microaggressive policies are intended to minimize the economic, political, and social impact of changing demographics from minority to majority

## Trump's Outreach via Political Microaggressions

In 2016, for a second straight year the number of hate groups in the United States continued to increase. According to the Southern Poverty Law Center (SPLC), since the candidacy of President Donald Trump radical right groups have continued to increase.[64] The number of hate groups increased from 892 in 2015 to 917 in 2016. Mark Potok, senior fellow and editor of the Intelligence Report, declared that the United States saw a resurgence of white nationalist groups because of Donald Trump's policies that reflect the values of white nationalists.[65] Trump's inflammatory rhetoric about Muslims, Latinos, and African Americans is problematic because it has been closely tied to an increase in hate crimes against these groups. For example, in the first 10 days of the Trump administration, the SPLC confirmed 867 hate-related incidents, of which 300 were against Muslims.[66] During the 2016 presidential campaign Trump publicly made microaggressive remarks about Muslims and during his first weeks in office signed Executive Order 13769 and revised Executive Order 13780, suspending the entry of Muslims from eight countries to the United States.

Donald Trump's use of microaggressions has provided a platform for supremacist groups who support antiminority rhetoric, which is problematic as demographics continue to change. As Jessie Daniels articulates in *White Lies*, elected officials at the highest levels of the U.S. government have used sedition to attract white supremacist organizations and have exerted very little effort to contest supremacist rhetoric.[67] When elected officials at all levels of government create a narrative of "us versus them," action ensues in the form of hate crimes.[68] The exacerbation of the "us versus them" framework results in the bifurcation of majority minority groups.

Take for example how political rhetoric is used to frame the "us versus them" scenario. On August 12, 2017, white nationalist and other alternative-right groups descended on Charlottesville, Virginia, for a Unite the Right rally. White nationalists marched in opposition to the city's removal of a statue of Confederate general Robert E. Lee. White nationalist, neo-Nazi, and Ku Klux Klan members were met by counterprotestors, and the rally turned violent and deadly. Twenty-year-old James Alex Fields Jr. of Ohio, a self-identified white nationalist, drove his vehicle into a crowd of anti–white nationalist protestors, injuring 19 individuals and killing Heather Heyer, an advocate for the marginalized. Also attending the white supremacy rally was David Duke, the former Imperial Wizard of the Ku Klux Klan and former Louisiana state representative. While at the Charlottesville rally, Duke participated in an on-camera interview:

> Interviewer: What does today represent to you, and the camera is right here, what does today represent to you?

Duke: This represents a turning point for the people of this country; we are determined to take our country back.

Duke: We are going to fulfil the promises of Donald Trump, that's what we believed in and that's why we voted for Donald Trump because he said he's going to take our country back and that's what we gotta do.[69]

Several hours after the violence erupted in Charlottesville, President Donald Trump tweeted his condemnation of hate and violence in America.[70] Two hours later Trump addressed the nation condemning the violence on many sides, but did not specifically condemn the actions of white nationalist and other alternative-right groups. In response to Trump's comments, David Duke tweeted the following:

I would recommend you take a good look in the mirror & remember it was White Americans who put you in the presidency, not radical leftists.[71]

Two days later, Duke followed up with these tweets:

The Alt-Right is a group of young White people who realise their future has been stolen, their culture subverted & their rights trampled on.[72]

We have the right to protest the purposeful demographic replacement of our people. We have a right to demand equal treatment.[73]

Three days after the violence in Charlottesville, Donald Trump appeared at a news conference to announce the signing of an executive order streamlining the process for infrastructure projects. However, Trump was immediately pressed on the events in Charlottesville. After some back and forth exchanges with the press, Trump was asked if he was putting the "alt-left and the alt-right" on the same moral plane. Trump responded:

And, you had some very bad people in that group, but you also have people that were very fine people, on both sides. You had people in that group, excuse me, excuse me. . . . You have people in that group that were there to protest taking down to them a very, very important statue, and renaming of a park from Robert E. Lee to another name. George Washington was a slave owner. . . . So will George Washington now lose his status? Are we going to take down, are we going to take down statues of George Washington? . . . You are changing history, you're changing culture.[74]

In this exchange, President Donald Trump states, "You are changing history, you're changing culture." These jarring remarks underscore the challenges minority groups will have as they transition from minority to majority. The majority group will not acquiesce to their economic, political, and social dominance without a psychological and physical battle. As the SPLC notes, Trump has publicly legitimized the idea and values of white supremacy. Add to this Trump's constant use of microaggressions to denigrate groups and the bifurcation between "us and them" is escalated to dangerous levels.

## Conclusion

The rapid proliferation of minority populations has the potential of changing government institutions, laws, and the political process. As a result, and to a degree, non-Hispanic whites are attuned to the changing ethnic balance and political environment precipitated by the growth in African American, Asian American, Latino, and immigrant populations. For some political elites and nativists, the awareness of changing demographics exacerbates the need to keep the United States monolithic. The natural inclination becomes protecting communities against growing minority groups that threaten American mores and values. Or, as Samuel Huntington puts forth in his highly controversial article "The Hispanic Challenge": "There is no American dream. There is only the American dream created by an Anglo Protestant society. Mexican Americans will share in that dream only if they dream in English."[75] This visceral nativist reaction is intended to homogenize what it means to be an American.

Perceptions of shifting political power are not a new phenomenon among nativists. Societal opposition toward immigrants has occurred throughout history. What may be unlike other occurrences in U.S. history is the rapid proliferation of Latino and Asian populations and the *possibility* of a transition to a majority-minority population. This possible transition may incite fear among some non-Hispanic white communities, resulting in hostile rhetoric and negative actions. Adding to the fear of changing demographics are elected officials who use political rhetoric to frame minority groups negatively, which escalates the already tense phenomenon of changing demographics and the "us versus them" scenario. As minority populations continue to grow, they will be confronted with opposition from some of those in the majority who will not willfully relinquish economic, political, and social control. Battle lines have been drawn and will not be easily crossed or erased. In an era of negative political rhetoric where certain groups of people are marginalized, changing demographics matter. More important, hostile political rhetoric, specifically microaggressions, matter in U.S. politics because this oratory is effective at setting a tone in which politicians and regular American citizens (e.g., family, friends, coworkers, church members) feel at ease marginalizing certain individuals and groups, which leads to discriminatory public policy that affect all citizens.

# CHAPTER THREE

# Political Discourse: Inflammatory Innuendos

On the night of June 3, 2017, the London Bridge terror attack occurred with a van hitting pedestrians and then continuing on to Borough Market where three suspected Islamic terrorists stabbed multiple people.[1] In response to the London terror attacks U.S. President Donald Trump tweeted the following: "We must stop being politically correct and get down to the business of security for our people. If we don't get smart it will only get worse."[2]

Throughout the history of the United States, political elites have used microaggressions to articulate their views along a spectrum of issues. Political elites frame their ideas in a manner that will appeal to voters or provide microaggression cues to incite fear, spatial distance, and feelings of superiority. By using microaggressions, political elites believe their message resonates with voters. They use microaggressions under the conviction that they are simply saying what "everyone else" is thinking but are too afraid to say. Because political elites believe they are saying what everyone else is thinking, those who oppose or reject the idea of microaggressions are seen as too politically correct or "soft." Perpetrators of microaggressions believe political correctness is associated with an attack on free speech and American culture.[3] As a result, the term *political correctness* is now used as a verbal weapon against those who oppose negative or hostile rhetoric. Recall that the definition of a microaggression is a direct, intentional, verbal, and divisive, comment, which communicates hostile, derogatory, or negative insults toward a person, group, or organization. As such, perpetrators support their own use of hostile rhetoric but object when microaggressions are used against them, their group, or organization. Perpetrators are okay with insulting or denigrating others, but they become uncomfortable when direct, hostile rhetoric is used against them personally. Perpetrators do not have an issue using microaggressions because they believe it is what "everyone" is thinking and saying, as long as no one is insulting them.

This is not to insinuate that all perpetrators of microaggression are not remorseful when they use hostile rhetoric or that supporters blindly accept the framing of the rhetoric by political elites. What is true is that although perpetrators may be remorseful and supporters do not necessarily "buy into" the rhetoric, both still engage with and accept the practice. Historically, microaggression cues in American politics have occurred because citizens tolerate them and because they accentuate differences between various groups in society and political elites. We need look no further than the 2016 U.S. presidential election between Republican Donald Trump and Democrat Hillary Clinton to illustrate how microaggression cues were used to differentiate the candidates. Republican candidate Donald Trump referred to Hillary Clinton as "crooked Hillary" and a "nasty woman." Clinton referred to Trump as temperamentally unfit to serve. Today's political microaggressions are not new to politics. The Founding Fathers engaged in microaggressive behavior when the United States was founded—these ideas were articulated in the documents that became the foundation of American democratic values. This chapter will examine microaggression cues from the Founding Fathers and current and former elected officials in local, state, and federal elections. This chapter will spend considerable time discussing interviews with public leaders and their views on the use of microaggressions, and when applicable, their responses to such cues. The chapter will also illustrate that negative political rhetoric in the form of microaggressions does matter, because it provides a platform for political elites and ordinary American citizens such as our friends, coworkers, family members, and religious leaders to openly disparage and discriminate against certain individuals and groups, which results in biased public policies.

## The Founding Fathers

The objective of this section is not to denounce or demean the figures who conceptualized American political institutions and the documents that have helped shape the republic, but to call attention to the use of political microaggressions by some of the most revered men in U.S. history. Regardless of how history is viewed, we must acknowledge the figures who conceptualized government in its various forms purposely enslaved individuals and excluded others from various founding documents (e.g., the Declaration of Independence and the U.S. Constitution). Although negative stereotypes about Native Americans, blacks, and immigrants were common attitudes of the era, it does not lessen the impact microaggressions had on recipients or their problematic nature. Moreover, the examples that follow will illustrate that negative rhetoric has and continues to be used to create an environment where political figures and regular American citizens feel comfortable engaging in political microaggressions with no recourse or consequence. While some may view political microaggressions as an acceptable practice, the end result is public policies not in the best interest of the majority of Americans.

Benjamin Franklin, one of the Founding Fathers of the United States and the only signatory to three of the founding documents (Declaration of Independence, the Treaty of Paris, and the U.S. Constitution) was born in 1706 in Boston, Massachusetts, a British colony. In 1723, Franklin left Boston and arrived in Pennsylvania, an American colony founded by William Penn. Upon his arrival, Franklin was alarmed to find ethnic and religious pluralism of English, German, and Swedish settlers and Quakers and English Anglicans coexisting in a relatively tolerant society.[4] After several years in Pennsylvania, Franklin was no longer able to conceal his increasing concern over the growing immigrant population. In response, Franklin wrote *Observation Concerning the Increase of Mankind*, a 24-point essay about the continued population growth in the new colonies.[5] Throughout the essay, Franklin is clear about his Eurocentric ideology and his views on slavery as an economic issue rather than a moral dilemma. In point 23, Franklin's political microaggressions are evident in his portrayal of Germans as:

> Palatine Boors [i.e., "hord of hogs"] that swarm into our Settlements, and by herding together establish their Language and Manners to the Exclusion of ours . . . Why should Pennsylvania, founded by the English, become a Colony of Aliens, who will shortly be so numerous as to Germanize us instead of our Anglifying them, and will never adopt our Language or Customs, any more than they can acquire our Complexion.[6]

The reinforcement of microaggression cues is illustrated by comparing Germans to "swarming hogs" who want to dominate Pennsylvania with their customs and language. Franklin goes on to remark that Germans will never assimilate to English customs much less attain the necessary complexion. Franklin's comments were destabilizing and problematic, since William Penn purposely encouraged immigration to Pennsylvania when he founded the colony.

In point 24, Franklin continues his use of microaggressions by stating that all "blacks and tawneys" should be excluded from America in order for the "white and red" population to increase.[7] Franklin was well regarded, and his writings were very persuasive during this era. However, Franklin's intentional microaggressions communicate his hostility toward immigrants and establishes the recurrent use of microaggressions by political figures. In this case, it is Franklin, an integral figure in the drafting of democratic documents, who creates an "us versus them" environment.

Thomas Jefferson—Founding Father, principal drafter of the Declaration of Independence, and third president of the United States—lived in an era when slavery and/or slave ownership was an accepted practice. Although Jefferson acknowledged that slaves served an economic purpose (i.e., cheaper labor) and enslaved over six hundred individuals, Jefferson opposed slavery and struggled with the institution and the ramifications of separating slave families.[8] Jefferson wrote *Notes on the State of Virginia* in 1787, reflecting on his work in the Virginia Assembly and his views on various issues. In *Notes* Jefferson was responding to a questionnaire he received while governor of Virginia from the secretary of the French legation to the United States, François Barbé-Marbois. *Notes* is a compilation of Jefferson's thoughts and views, including his observations of the geographical features of Virginia and a catalog of the birds of the state. However, in Query XIV, Jefferson discusses the emancipation of slaves and their removal from America. In this chapter, Jefferson acknowledges that interactions between whites and blacks are tolerable, but anything other than an interaction should be considered unnatural.[9] Throughout the chapter, Jefferson discusses his concern over emancipation and how it could lead to divisions within the state because of deep-rooted prejudicial attitudes by whites.[10] In a subtle microaggressive insult, Jefferson writes "comparing them [blacks/slaves] by their faculties of memory, reason, and imagination, it appears to me that in memory they are equal to the whites; in reason much inferior . . . and that in imagination they are dull, tasteless, and anomalous."[11] Throughout Query XIV, Jefferson reiterates his view that blacks are inferior to whites in body and mind.[12] Although these comments were the popular thought of this era, Jefferson exemplifies the perpetual use of microaggressions by political elites. Much like Franklin, Jefferson was well regarded and was a very influential writer during this period. Support for Jefferson's repatriation philosophy and the shared sentiment that blacks were inferior to whites can be found through the establishment of the American Colonization Society in 1816, an organization that argued that slaves would never be able to integrate into American society. This same sentiment can be found in the writings of James Buchanan, Henry Clay, Andrew Jackson, and Abraham Lincoln.

Another influential political figure who engaged in the use of political microaggressions during a pivotal era in American history was Abraham Lincoln. Lincoln—elected to the U.S. presidency in 1860 and known for trying to preserve the Union—while broaching the subject of emancipation during the Civil War was revered in the Northeast and Northwest but was an unpopular figure in the Southern states.[13] Ultimately, the Union was victorious over the Confederate states, and Lincoln issued the Emancipation Proclamation, which was instrumental in the ratification of the Thirteenth

Amendment abolishing slavery.[14] However, prior to issuing the Emancipation Proclamation, Lincoln held stereotypic views about blacks. Similar to Jefferson's writings, Lincoln's views were the popular thought of this era, yet he still engaged in political microaggressions. More significant, Lincoln articulated his views about blacks in his debate with Stephen A. Douglas.

The 1858 Illinois senatorial debates between Abraham Lincoln and Stephen A. Douglas illustrate the use of hostile rhetoric to cue supporters. Early in his political career, Abraham Lincoln was a member of the Republican Party, also referred to as the "Black Republican" party by Democrats because of its members' "espousal of the rights of the negro."[15] Stephen Douglas, the incumbent Democrat senator from Illinois, supported the expansion of slavery in U.S. territory. The first of seven debates was a contentious affair; Douglas dominated the forum by accusing Lincoln of being an abolitionist (someone who favors abolishing slavery) and the candidate who favored racial equality.[16] Douglas cued voters by stating that Lincoln was a "deserter of Democracy" and someone who opposed the Dred Scott decision.[17] (In *Dred Scott v. Sandford* (1957), Chief Justice Taney of the U.S. Supreme Court wrote in his opinion that slaves from Africa were not U.S. citizens and thus could not sue for their freedom.) The use of political microaggression cues is evident in the exchange between the two candidates and their views on the expansion of slavery. Douglas, in his opening remarks, relies on hostile rhetoric and accusations about Lincoln's position on slavery to cue his supporters:

> I desire to know whether Mr. Lincoln to-day stands, as he did in 1854, in favor of the unconditional repeal of the Fugitive Slave law. I desire him to answer whether he stands pledged to-day, as he did in 1854, against the admission of any more Slave States into the Union, even if people want them.[18]
>
> Do you desire to strike out of our State Constitution that clause which keeps slaves and free negroes out of the State, and allow the free negroes to flow in, and cover your prairies with black settlements? Do you desire to turn this beautiful State into a free negro colony, in order that when Missouri abolishes slavery she can send one hundred thousand emancipated slaves into Illinois, to become citizens and voters, on an equality with yourself? . . . For one, I am opposed to negro citizenship in any and every form. I believe this Government was made on white basis. I believe it was made by white men, for the benefit of white men and their posterity forever, and I am in favor of confining citizenship to white men, men of European birth and descent, instead of conferring it upon negroes, Indians, and other inferior race.[19]

Although Lincoln believed slavery was wrong, he was forced into defensive posturing and responded by stating that his political views had been misrepresented. In the first debate, Lincoln was asked seven questions, none of which he addressed; instead, he found himself having to denounce Douglas's allegations:

> When a man hears himself somewhat misrepresented, it provokes him.—
> at least, I find it so with myself; but when misrepresentation becomes very
> gross and palpable, it is more apt to amuse him. . . . I have no purpose to
> introduce political and social equality between the white and the black
> races. There is a physical difference between the two which, in my judge-
> ment, will probably forever forbid their living together upon the footing of
> perfect equality; and inasmuch as it becomes a necessity there must be a
> difference, I, as well as Judge Douglas, am in favor of the race to which I
> belong having the superior position.[20]

Political microaggressions were in full force in the first Illinois senatorial debate. Although Douglas's comments were the popular thought of the era, he still demeans slaves as a group and considers them lesser human beings by stating "I am opposed to negro citizenship in any and every form. I believe this Government was made on white basis." Similarly, Lincoln responds with his own political microaggression when he states "I, as well as Judge Douglas, am in favor of the race to which I belong having the superior position." This intentional comment marginalized slaves as individuals outside of social desirability. As is evident from the writings of Benjamin Franklin, Thomas Jefferson, and the 1858 senatorial debates between Lincoln and Douglas, political elites, elected officials, and political candidates have relied on negative cues to rally supporters. Many of the other Founding Fathers shared similar views to those of Franklin, Jefferson, and Lincoln and used microaggressions to rally support and negatively frame certain groups. Moreover, this line of reasoning would continue for another hundred years, before microaggressions were addressed through civil rights legislation. Even as the United States has evolved into the twenty-first century, some elected officials continue to use microaggressions and hold negative views about African Americans, Latinos, Asians, and most recently Muslims.

## Unrestrained Microaggressions

The claim in this study is twofold: one, speech in the form of a microaggression is used as a weapon in a changing racial and ethnic environment. Groups that have held the majority of elected positions may be uncomfortable with changing demographics, leading to microaggressions. Two, the continuous use of negative political rhetoric, specifically microaggressions, matters in U.S. politics. Fundamentally, hostile rhetoric used as a weapon creates a divisive environment where members of a community feel comfortable discriminating against certain individuals and groups, which results in policies that are not in the best interest of 99 percent of the American people. A full analysis of the components and effects of microaggressions is beyond the scope of this chapter; instead the focus is on showing how microaggressions occur at all levels of government and how changing demographics are feared by some of those who have historically held economic, political, and cultural majorities. This chapter will also provide an examination of how victims of microaggressions react and how the reaction of perpetrators is an important component for understanding how effective microaggressions can be and, if met head-on, how ineffective hostile rhetoric is.

Studies indicate groups accustomed to being in dominant political, economic, and social positions will use microaggressions when they can exploit and manipulate differences between groups while simultaneously using their power to frame subordinate groups as unambitious and threatening.[21] Following are multiple accounts of how microaggressions are used in government settings by elected officials and by the majority who view the election of some minorities as unwelcoming and a threat to the community. Interviews were conducted with current and former local, state, and federally elected officials. Of the 125 randomly selected current and former elected officials, 23 agreed to be interviewed, for a response rate of 18.4 percent. Of the 23 current and former elected officials who agreed to participate in the survey, nine were from local government, eight were elected to state offices, four were elected to the U.S. House of Representatives, and two were elected to the U.S. Senate.[22] Analysis of interviews with local, state, and federally elected government officials revealed that the use of microaggressions was a common occurrence at all levels of government. Interview data suggests that the use of political microaggressions is more common when race and gender are a factor. The use of political microaggressions reveals that when compared to non-Hispanic whites, minorities elected to offices in areas predominantly politically controlled by non-Hispanic whites are more likely to be recipients of microaggressions. These findings seem to confirm the assertion that some non-Hispanic whites are uncomfortable with changing demographics.

## Microaggressions in Local Government

When minorities are elected to local government offices, the use of political microaggressions increases. Minorities elected to offices historically controlled by non-Hispanic whites are more likely to be recipients of microaggressions. Moreover, if the elected official is female and minority, the use of political and general microaggressions also increases. The findings from elected officials in local and state government confirm that some non-Hispanic whites continue to hold stereotypic views regarding race and gender.

For instance, County Commissioner A, who is a minority in a small, conservative Texas town, shared his view about his election to the county: "In regard to racism, nothing has improved, it's just hidden better." When asked specifically if the commissioner was aware of the use of political microaggression by other elected officials, the commissioner stated "Yes, I've known about it for a long time, I just call 'em insults." The commissioner reasserted his view on the use of political microaggressions at higher levels of government by stating, "That kinda language is not sustainable, you have to learn to keep your cool, if you keep talking like that you'll keep your base [supporters], but nothing more." When asked, "What is the most prevalent or problematic microaggression issue in your area?" the commissioner responded, "My race or race in this small town is still a problem."

County Commissioner B in Floyd County, Texas, who has been politically active for over 40 years, expressed his views on political microaggressions by stating, "Yeah, call it what you want, racism is still here." When asked, "Prior to this interview, were you aware of the use of political microaggressions by elected officials?" Commissioner B responded with, "Yes." When probed a little more on what specifically he was referring to and whether he thought microaggressions were always racial comments, Commissioner B shared the following story:

> When I was in grade school I knew how to speak English and Spanish. In my class, there were two other Mexicanos in the class, so when the teacher would tell us to do something, the two Mexicanos would look at me and I would tell them what the teacher had said, but in Spanish. One day the teacher pulls me aside and says [name], where did you learn to speak English? I said at home. So, then the teacher asks me does your mother speak English? And I said yes. I guess the teacher was confused because then she asked me if my father spoke English and again I said yes. Well I guess my explanation was not enough for her because she then asked me what do you speak at home, and I said English and Spanish. And the teacher says, oh, when did your family cross the river? I'm looking at her thinking what river? So I say well there is a little creek close to our house and we cross over it. Then the teacher says when did your parents cross over? Were you born there and had to cross or were you born here after your family crossed? At this point, I was so confused because at the time I had no idea what she was talking about. I went home and told my mom about what the teacher had asked me and my mom [the use of profanity] cussed the teacher out. My mom told me, go back tomorrow and tell your teacher that you were born in Colorado and we did not cross over to get here, we have been here. It was not until I turned 15 that I understood what had happened in grade school.

Commissioner B recognizes that he has been the recipient of microaggressions for a very long time, but to him the direct, intentional, hostile, derogatory, and negative insults have always been framed from a racial perspective.

Recall from Chapter 1 that microaggressions are also microassaults equating to "old-fashioned racism." When asked directly about his experience as an elected official and if he has ever been the target of a political microaggression, Commissioner B explains:

> This is what I hate about this town, they want the Mexicans to be very patriotic, but if it's a gringa [white woman] that has to go out and put up the flag in city hall, they don't want to do it, but if they have a Mexicano do it, then it's okay. They think we are all dirty Mexicans, but at the same time, they want us to be patriotic and salute the flag, they can't have it both ways.

Commissioner B's stance on political microaggressions was straightforward and unequivocal. As a commissioner and a citizen in a small conservative town, he has experienced microassaults at various levels. From the commissioner's perspective, the microassaults he has experienced are based on how Latinos in the community are framed. Eduardo Bonilla-Silva defines cultural racism as a frame that is based on culturally based arguments to explain the position of certain groups in society.[23] In this case, "dirty Mexicans" is the cultural view held by some in this small conservative West Texas town. Commissioner B went on to say: "Since I've been politically active since the 1970s and I worked with groups such as Chicanos Unidos-Campesinos, La Raza, and the Brown Berets, this kind of stuff is not new. Like I said, from the time I was in grade school people have been making these kinds of comments." To put the commissioner's comments about race into perspective, according to the 2010 Census, 53 percent of the population in Floyd County identify as Latino. More than half the population is Latino, and according to Commissioner B's accounts they are stereotyped as "dirty Mexicans" by some members of the community. Denigrating half of the population in a county is a classic microassault or "old-fashioned racism."

Another variation of a microaggression is a microinvalidation. This type of microaggression is an uninformed and uneducated action that occurs outside the awareness of the perpetrator.[24] These types of verbal comments or behaviors minimize marginalized groups.[25] The following is an example of a microinvalidation in local government and illustrates how a female Latina serving in local government was the recipient of a microinvalidation based on her gender and ethnicity. When asked, "Prior to this interview, were you aware of the use of political microaggressions?" Commissioner C stated:

> As a county commissioner for the county, we were working on sorting out some issues and we had a meeting with several members of the city council and other board members. I get to the meeting and as usual I am the only Latina in the room. After a while a high-end mediation attorney from

Dallas comes in to run the meeting and hands me a stack of papers and says, "Can you go make me some copies?" I responded, sir, I am one of the two voting members of the committee and I would be more than happy to make you copies if you would like. The attorney turned bright red and it was our city attorney that jumped out of his chair and said I'll get those copies for you.

In the exchange shared by Commissioner C the classic microinvalidation is the assumption that the only Latina in the room must be the secretary or administrative assistant for someone else in the room; thus, it is acceptable to ask her to make copies. In this account, it never occurred to the attorney that the only Latina in the room was one of two voting members of the meeting. The attorney's preconceived, uninformed, and uneducated behavior and thoughts occurred outside his awareness. In this case, the attorney from Dallas held a stereotypic view of Latinas, which when confronted caused him to feel uneasy (we can infer this since Commissioner C stated the "attorney turned bright red" during the exchange). This type of microinvalidation minimizes marginalized groups to emphasize that they are at a lower economic, political, and social hierarchical level. This exchange confirms the research by Derald Wing Sue on how minority groups are seen as existing on the margins of society.

Groups that are marginalized in society exist on the lower and or outer limits of social desirability and consciousness. Minorities regardless of race, ethnicity, LGBT status, women, and those with disabilities are perceived negatively, given less status in society, and confined to existing on the margins of our social, cultural, political and economic systems. The result is often exclusion from the mainstream of life in our society, unequal treatment, and social inequality. The inferior status and treatment associated with marginality are constant, continuing, and cumulative experiences of socially devalued groups.[26]

Council member A (a non-Hispanic white) was elected to his post in a city in Iowa two years ago. Council member A was asked, "Prior to this interview, were you aware of the use of political microaggressions by elected officials?" The immediate response was "No," followed by "How do you define a political what-did-you-call-it?" After discussing microaggressions with Council member A, he reiterated, "No, I have not heard or participated in microaggressions while in office." When asked about his position on the use of political microaggressions by elected officials, Council member A stated, "I don't think insults of any kind have a place in politics. Listen, I have a meeting to get to and will have to end this interview." Similarly, Council member B from a small Montana town and Council member C from Louisiana expressed almost identical responses to Council member A; neither had heard or participated in microaggressions while in office. When asked about their position on the use of political microaggressions by elected officials, both B and C indicated that they were not aware of the use of microaggressions and terminated their interviews.

Council member A represents middle-income households in a city in North Carolina. Council member A has served as part of the city council for five years. To the question, "Prior to this interview, were you aware of the use of political microaggressions by elected officials?" she responded, "Darling, I'm not sure what you mean by microaggressions." After a discussion on microaggressions, Council member A stated the following:

> Oh, yes, I have heard all kinds of crazy things since I was elected. Here in the South, sometimes it's difficult to change the attitudes of certain people. For the most part, everyone on the council treats me fine, but I have had those occasional comments from the men, did you bake any cookies or how does [husband's name] survive when we have these late meetings. Implying that I should be taking care of my husband rather than serving the community.

When probed on "What is the best way to deal with political microaggression?" Council member A laughed and said: "Well it depends on what the comment is. Most of the time I remind them that they have wives and if they want cookies to ask them to bake 'em. You have to understand, they are just trying to be funny and they are not trying to insult me."

What is interesting about this account is that earlier, Council member A stated she had "heard some crazy things and in the South, sometimes it's difficult to change the attitudes," but in the follow-up questions when she was asked about the best way to deal with political microaggressions, Council member A seemed to backtrack from her original response in an effort to minimize the potential negative view about her colleagues. In a follow-up question, "Have you ever heard a specific political microaggression used by a member of the council?" "Sure, I've heard some things, but I don't think they really mean them. I'm not making excuses for them, it's just sometimes people say things without thinking."

In Council member A's response, she was both a victim of a microaggression and a perpetrator of a microaggression. In the first case, she was the recipient of a microinvalidation, the assumption that as a female it is her responsibility to bake for the remaining council members. Second, by excusing the microaggressions of her colleagues she too becomes a perpetrator of the cyclical nature of microaggressions.

## Responding to Microaggressions in Local Government

In order to adequately understand the totality of microaggressions, we need to also examine how recipients of a microaggression respond to hostile rhetoric. As discussed in Chapter 1 microaggressions are verbal, behavioral, and environmental insults, which take the form of microinsults, microassaults, and microinvalidations.[27] Research by Derald Wing Sue and colleagues on the psychological effects of microaggressions found recipients of microaggressions experience several reactions ranging from a clash of racial realities, where whites and African Americans view race relations and interactions differently, to the Catch-22 where victims contemplate "Did that really just happen?" and the conflict between the benefits of responding versus negative consequences.[28] Regardless of the reaction, microaggressions have a significant negative psychological effect on marginalized groups in communities.[29] In interviews with locally elected government officials who have been the recipients of microaggressions at least in local government, they rebuke their perpetrators. While examining the psychological impact to elected officials is outside the purview of this research, we can still draw considerable insight from elected officials on how recipients and perpetrators of microaggressions react to verbal, behavioral, and environmental insults.

In a follow-up question with local elected officials about the best way to deal with political microaggressions, several respondents articulated similar experiences with dealing with perpetrators. When asked, "What is the best way to deal with political microaggressions?" Commissioner A stated: "I challenge a lot of things here—in fact, I think more people have started to respect me because I do challenge what they say and the comments they make. People are finally realizing that they have to accept me regardless, cause I'm here to stay." Commissioner A's answer, particularly his comment "people are finally realizing that they have to accept me regardless, cause I'm here to stay," could easily go unnoticed or considered as progress in race relations in the community. However, at the onset of the interview in discussing biographical information, Commissioner A recalled his early experience in local government by expressing how negatively some in the community viewed his election to the city council. Commissioner A stated, "When I first ran for city council years ago, 'they' decided to put a choke hold on me and 'they' were successful in putting a choke hold on me." When probed on who "they" were, Commissioner A responded, "The whites." From Commissioner A's responses, it is difficult to determine if people in his community are becoming more receptive to his election in local government or if the exchange between the perpetrators of microaggressive insults and Commissioner A's challenges have become the norm, creating a false narrative of respect and acceptance. Although the intent of some members of the community is ambiguous, Commissioner A's response is clear: he challenges microaggressions.

Similarly, Commissioner B was asked the same question, "What is the best way to deal with political microaggressions?" he responded, "When I was on the city council and now that I'm on the commissioner's court, any little racial comment I hear I attack right away. I let them know that I won't stand for it." Commissioner B went on to state that he is not the only target of microaggressions by other elected officials; he expressed his concern over citizens in the community as recipients of microaggressions:

> I challenged the sheriff two or three months ago at one of our commissioner's meetings where he was giving us an update on several things, "You gave 96 tickets and 60 were to Hispanics and 36 to Anglos, why the difference?" Remember, right now, we have four Hispanics on the sheriff's department. The sheriff said there are more Hispanics, and I said bullshit don't tell me that, we are only 63 percent Hispanic. I told the JP who is a good friend of mine, there are four officers in the county that are Hispanics and when they pull someone Anglo over they've been told don't give them a ticket, but give the Mexicans a ticket, that way it doesn't look like racial profiling when you have Mexican cops giving Mexicans tickets.

Commissioner B stated, "any little racial comment I hear I attack right away," and then gave an account of how he believes the justice system is also riddled with individuals asked to propagate microaggressive behavior against citizens. Microaggressions are not limited to vertical one-on-one interactions. Microaggressions can also be mandated by individuals with power over others: in this case, a superior and a subordinate. Again, we have a case where an elected official confronts a perpetrator and the use of overt microaggressions.

Commissioner C was also asked, "What is the best way to deal with political microaggressions?" Commissioner C responded, "If there is discourse, I will confront." The Commissioner followed up her statement by stating: "Obviously, I look and sound very different, I am a young woman and Latina—I'm not sure that it has anything to do with it, but I am the only Latina female in a room full of white men; this changes the atmosphere." Recall, previously Commissioner C had been the recipient of a classic microinvalidation in her meeting with colleagues and the Dallas-based mediation attorney. The attorney mistakenly assumed Commissioner C was the administrative assistant for the meeting. Prior research argues that microinvalidations are often unconscious actions and occur outside the awareness of the perpetrator—this form of microaggression is the most harmful because verbal comments or behaviors negate the views of people of color.[30] However, stereotyping occurs within the consciousness of the perpetrator, which in this case would support the claim that perpetrators are aware of their use of microaggressions to denigrate others. When examined as a whole, there is a pattern where race and gender are a factor in microaggressive behavior in local government. In the accounts above, the commissioners responded with a willingness to unequivocally confront microaggressions targeted at them.

## Microaggressions in State Government

In this next section, microaggressions in state government are examined. In this part of the analysis, the responses are quite different when compared to the responses from local government officials. Eight officials elected to state offices were interviewed as part of the analysis on the use of microaggressions by political elites. Of the eight individuals who were interviewed, two were female, six were male, and all were non-Hispanic white. Six of the eight interviewees only answered one question, "Prior to this interview, were you aware of the use of political microaggression cues by elected officials?" The two remaining individuals answered two questions each. None of the eight interviewees was familiar with the term *microaggression*.

State official C: "Prior to this interview, were you aware of the use of political microaggressions by elected officials?"

Sure, after you defined the term, I have heard other colleagues at the state use insults and make questionable comments about certain groups. But listen, it is not intentional, and I don't think they really mean what they say. Sometimes, we all say things that in retrospective we wish we would not have said. Now if you will excuse me, I have to grab the other line.

State official E: "Prior to this interview, were you aware of the use of political microaggressions by elected officials?"

Well, prior to this interview I was not aware of the term *microaggression* used to describe, basically, rude comments. So, yes, I have heard microaggressions used by other elected officials and by my constituents. I won't go into the details about the comments. We as elected officials represent our constituents and our state, and we should move away from this tendency to insult each other. I represent all my constituents evenly and to the best of my ability. Everyone else elected to public office should strive for the same.

State official F: "Prior to this interview, were you aware of the use of political microaggressions by elected officials?"

Thank you for clarifying political microaggressions. I can't say I've heard microaggressions in my limited time in office. I do think sometimes society has become a little overly sensitive, especially when the media jumps on any little sound bite. But it is no excuse for using language, language that creates doubts about a situation.

State official F: "What is the best way to deal with political microaggression cues?"

I think it starts with educating folks about issues [interview ended].

The responses from elected officials C, E, and F indicate they have all heard the use of microaggressions while serving in office. However, notice how the officials make a qualifying statement about the use of microaggressions. Official C states that the insults are not intentional. Recall from Chapter 1 that perpetrators of microaggressions frame insults as harmless, inoffensive, and nonracially motivated. This type of microaggression is often less obvious, but just as powerful in its negative effect on the recipient. Official E brushes over the use of microaggressions and instead deflects the question to how constituents should be represented and comments that constituents have used microaggressions, but there was no indication if Official E addressed the use of microaggressions by constituents. This is an example of a microinvalidation, where denigrating comments or behaviors invalidate how people feel. Official E obfuscated the question, by responding in the affirmative that he had heard the use of microaggressions—but no other remarks were offered on the subject. Official F argued that there was no excuse for using language that creates doubts. But, Official F previously stated that society was becoming overly sensitive. This illustrates how some individuals engage in the use of microaggressions as a justification by implying that they are saying what "everyone else" is thinking but is too afraid to say. Individuals who oppose or reject the use of microaggressions are seen as too politically correct, or in this case, "overly sensitive."

Elected officials A and D each responded to two questions: "Prior to this interview, were you aware of the use of political microaggressions by elected officials, and what is the best way to deal with political microaggression?"

State official A: No, I am not aware of microaggressions or if my colleagues engage in such behavior. The best way to deal with this kind of problem is to push back against, what is it again, microaggression?

Interviewer: Yes, a microaggression.

State official A: Sometimes you have to be thick-skinned and let it roll off and other times you have to address the comment right away. I'm sure that my colleagues are not intentionally trying to hurt or stereotype folks.

State official D: As a female in a male-dominated world, I've heard all kinds of comments. But, as a woman you can't overreact or show hurt feelings. In politics, once your "friends" sense a weakness they will try and expose it.

For me, the best way to deal with microaggressions is to nip it in the bud. I call out my male colleagues and let them know comments about my gender are not acceptable. You have to have the right tone, and timing is everything. Politics can be very short-lived, so knowing when to call out people is a balancing act.

From the account of State official A, he is not aware of the use of microaggressions in politics, but his response is somewhat contradictory. First, Official A denies the use of microaggressions, and then second, he states "sometimes you have to be thick-skinned and let it roll off and other times you have to address the comment right away. I'm sure that my colleagues are not intentionally trying to hurt or stereotype folks." This indicates that Official A may be aware of the use of microaggressions, and, much like Official F, he believes that society is becoming overly sensitive and makes an excuse for his colleagues' actions. Similarly, Official D also mentions that "timing is everything." Since we did not pose the question about timing, it is difficult to determine when the appropriate time is to address microaggressions by perpetrators. Official D's answer suggests that females in elected office are recipients of microaggressions by their male colleagues. Notice how Official D qualifies her statement of "I call out my male colleagues" by saying "timing is everything." Can the low number of women in state elected offices be attributed to the high number of microaggressions toward them? Alternatively, do microaggressions increase when the elected official is a minority female? Based on these responses, the case can be made that gender and race are factors in the use of microaggressions by other elected officials. Moreover, does using caution or "picking the right time" provide an opportunity for microaggressions to continue?

Although the response rate and sample size are small, we can still extract valuable information. At least in this study of locally elected officials and state elected officials, the responses indicate that in local government recipients of microaggressions are more likely to confront perpetrators about their remarks, when compared to state officials. More important, based on the responses, minorities are more likely to challenge perpetrators on their use of microaggressions when compared to male non-Hispanic whites, indicating that minorities in public office are more attuned to negative comments and are willing to confront their perpetrators in order to remove or minimize barriers and obstacles to progress, in the diversification of the political process.

## Microaggressions in Congress

Members of the U.S. Congress represent constituents throughout the United States. Elected officials wield significant power in structuring and orchestrating public policy that affects the entire nation. As such, we would expect that representatives from the House and Senate would approach their role in government in an unobtrusive manner. As part of the interview process on the use of microaggressions by political elites, four members of the U.S. House of Representatives and two members from the U.S. Senate agreed to participate in interviews. However, as Senator B and Representative D cautioned, this may not be the best time to interview members on microaggressions. As a follow-up, Senator B and Representative D were asked "Why the caution?" and both had similar replies along the lines of "The current political climate requires us to carefully consider our responses—we do not all want to be portrayed as supporting the inflammatory discourse of this administration." Senator B and Representative D acknowledged the use of microaggressions by other elected officials, but did not want to elaborate on the comments. They were then asked, "What is the best way to deal with political microaggressions?" Representative D stated, "If I knew the answer, we would have a different administration." Senator B replied, "That's a great question, and we're still trying to figure out a response." Although the responses were brief, they are meaningful since they provide a window into the highest ranks in government. Neither had a solution for how to deal with microaggressions, but what was apparent was their frustration at the continued use of microaggressions by individuals at higher levels of government.

Representatives A, B, and C agreed to participate in the interviews, but after we posed the first question "Prior to this interview, were you aware of the use of microaggressions by elected officials?" all three declined to respond. Representatives A, B, and C were then asked a second question, "What is the best way to deal with microaggressions?"

Representative A: It depends on the comment and who makes the comment. There are times when comments can be misconstrued and at other times comments are more flippant with no direct target in mind.

Representative B: You tell me. What have others said?

Representative C: Hmm, here in the House we can be pretty blunt with each other. If I felt someone knowingly insulted me or my constituents, I would be just as blunt.

Senator A was also asked, "Prior to this interview, were you aware of the use of microaggressions by elected officials?"

Ma'am I don't mean to be rude, is this what you're really after? If you want me to say I've heard other members use microaggressions then the answer is "Yes." Politics is heated and sometimes it can get crass and things are said out of exasperation. No ill intent—it is just a way to get a point across.

The responses from House and Senate members were direct and to the point. From their remarks, they acknowledge the use of microaggressions and, similar to the responses from individuals elected to state offices, Congressional members qualified their acknowledgement of microaggressions. The following qualifiers were used: "comments can be misconstrued," "here in the House we can be pretty blunt," and "politics is heated and sometimes it can get crass." This indicates that at times microaggressions are acceptable practice for some members of Congress. Furthermore, Representative C also stated he retaliated against insults by being "just as blunt." Does responding in like manner create an atmosphere where microaggressions used to denigrate colleagues spill over to microaggressions used against groups outside of politics? In addition, what is the impact of microaggressions to changing demographics in the Congress? In the 114th Congress only 104 women served (84 in the House and 20 in the Senate), for an average of 19.4 percent of all members. Although significant progress has been made in the election of women to the House and Senate, are the continued use of microaggressions a result of an insulated, white-male-dominated "good old boys' club?" These are areas that will require additional research to fully understand the implications of microaggressions and changing demographics at the highest level of elected government.

## Conclusion

These findings are consistent with the claim argued in this research that microaggressions are deliberate and conscious views used by perpetrators, unlike other research that argues microaggressions are typically unconscious views of inclusion, exclusion, superiority, and inferiority negatively impacting the recipient.[31] The use of microaggressions was acknowledged by 82 percent of respondents at various levels of government. In state and federal government, where all the respondents were non-Hispanic white, the majority of respondents acknowledged the use of microaggressions and qualified the use of microaggressions by inserting statements such as "They are trying to be funny and they are not trying to insult me," "I've heard some things, but I don't think they really mean them," and "Society has become a little overly sensitive." These qualifying statements indicate there is significant latitude on the use of microaggressions. When colleagues excuse the behavior, then the behavior becomes the acceptable norm. While the overall sample size of respondents was small, there is enough evidence to support the claim that microaggressions are intentional and within the scope of consciousness of perpetrators.

More significant, the findings illustrate that minorities elected to local office are more willing to challenge the use of microaggressions by perpetrators. Minorities were willing to openly confront the use of microaggressions in numerous settings such as council meetings, commissioner's meetings, and other formal occasions where other individuals witness the exchange. This could be a substantial finding as demographics continue to change and more minorities are elected to office. Those who have held the majority and are accustomed to engaging in microaggressive behavior will be met with swift and direct challenges from changing demographics. The growing change in racial and gender demographics will create psychological dilemmas for those in the majority because of their resistance to change and the reality of what is already occurring. To sum up the survey, political rhetoric infused with microaggressions does matter, because it creates an atmosphere of misguided perceptions and stereotypes about certain individuals and groups—all of which lead to public policies that are not in the best interest of most Americans.

# CHAPTER FOUR

# Nativist Attitudes: American Minority Groups as Targets

On June 17, 2015, Dylann S. Roof, a white supremacist, killed nine African American parishioners at Emanuel African Methodist Episcopal Church, a historic black church in Charleston, South Carolina. Mr. Roof entered the church and Reverend Clementa C. Pinckney invited him to take a seat for a weekly Bible study. Mr. Roof sat with the group for about 40 minutes and when the group bowed for a benediction, Mr. Roof wielded a .45-caliber semiautomatic handgun and shot the parishioners. Victims were shot multiple times with over 70 shell casings scattered throughout the church. In his jailhouse manifesto, Mr. Roof confessed to the killings and expressed no remorse for his actions. Almost two years after the shootings, Mr. Roof was found guilty of 33 federal criminal charges, including hate crimes, and sentenced to death.[1]

On April 18, 2017, Kori Ali Muhammad was arrested in Fresno, California, for opening fire on unsuspecting white victims. Mr. Muhammad fired 16 rounds in 60 to 90 seconds, killing three white men. Police labeled the killings as unprovoked attacks and as a hate crime solely motivated by race. The police, in their statement to the press, indicated that Mr. Muhammad wanted to kill as many white men as he could before going to jail for a murder he previously committed.[2]

Recall from Chapter 1 that microassaults are a variation of microaggressions, which are often conscious, intentional biased beliefs or attitudes expressed primarily by a violent verbal or nonverbal attack meant to hurt a marginalized person or group. A microassault is "old-fashioned racism," where an action is conscious and deliberate. In this chapter, we will examine nativist attitudes as a form of microaggressions against African Americans, Asians, Latinos, and Muslims. Political rhetoric by public officials often frames how individuals view policy issues and, more importantly, how they respond to each other. Because political rhetoric is framed by elected officials, negative political discourse is an important issue that requires examination. Microaggressions by political elites create conditions where regular American citizens normalize the use of stereotypes and discriminatory practices, leading to public policies oftentimes affecting the majority of the population, not the wealthiest 1 percent of households. Consider research by Joe Feagin in which he examines white racial framing and systematic racism in the United States; he notes that "deeply imbedded beliefs and attitudes are constantly reflected in the talk and actions of everyday life. One need not know or accept the entire frame for it to have a substantial impact on thought and action. Each person may utilize selected elements of the dominant frame."[3]

Today, as in the past, political rhetoric can frame policy issues, individuals, and groups in positive or negative undertones. Political framing provides a heuristic shortcut for how people view and interact with each other. For example, in the 2016 presidential election, negative political rhetoric framed how voters viewed the Republican and Democratic candidates: the former as unhinged and the latter as a criminal. Although political elections are not for the fainthearted, the rhetoric in the 2016 presidential election galvanized a popular base and spurned others. History shows that political rhetoric has been used as a microaggression resulting in a conscious and deliberate microassault or old-fashioned racism.

In the United States, hate crimes committed against minority groups are not a new phenomenon. Hate crimes can be traced back to the Founding Fathers and the colonization of the United States. As Joe Feagin points out, although the Founding Fathers are revered for their moral fortitude and stance on liberty, most accepted the subjugation of blacks and the killing of Native Americans.[4] The Founding Fathers colluded to create a system that purposely favored one racial group over another. Founding U.S. documents such as the Declaration of Independence and the Constitution of the United States were written so that racial separation and oppression were maintained.[5] Clarence Lusane notes in his historical account of blacks in the White House that 12 former U.S. presidents, some revered as Founding Fathers (Washington, Jefferson, Madison, Monroe, Jackson, Van Buren, Harrison, Tyler, Polk, Taylor, Johnson, and Grant), were slaveholders at one time or another.[6] Of the 12 U.S. presidents who enslaved individuals, eight owned slaves while serving in office.[7] Thomas Jefferson, a leading architect of the Declaration of Independence and third president of the United States, was also a slaveholder who fathered slave children and took punitive measures against runaway slaves.[8] History also shows the complicit attempt at total genocide of Native Americans[9] and the lynching of African Americans,

Latinos, and Asian Americans as a form of punishment,[10] which established a system where jurisprudence was based on race. In essence, elected officials and the U.S. government have played an explicit role in perpetrating micro-aggressive crimes[11] against various group for centuries. The outlet for nativism is hate crimes against the groups infringing on the majority's economic, political, and social sphere. As such, numerous groups have been targets of hate crimes based on the foundation created by the Founding Fathers.

## Nativism and Microaggressions

A hate crime is a "criminal offense against a person or property motivated in whole or in part by an offender's bias against a race, religion, disability, sexual orientation, ethnicity, gender, or gender identity."[12] The Uniform Crime Reporting (UCR) Program distinguishes between hate crime incidents and offenses. An incident "is one in which one or more offense types are motivated by the same bias."[13] Offenses are defined as crimes against persons and property; they include murder, rape, aggravated assault, intimidation, robbery, arson, and several other forms of crime.[14] This research utilizes the latter categorization in order to capture individual criminal offenses against African Americans, Asians, Latinos, and Muslims.

With this in mind, there are four significant limitations to the number of reported hate crimes and the collection of estimation data. First, the FBI requires states and local governments to collect and report hate crime data. The FBI is reliant on voluntarily compliance by states and local governments to report such data.[15] Voluntary compliance means that some jurisdictions may not report hate crime offenses. Second, the data is contingent on victims reporting hate crime incidents and offenses.[16] Third, law enforcement are given latitude to categorize hate crimes as either an incident and/or offense based on individual subjectivity.[17] Because of the subjectivity in classifying hate crimes, in 2015, over 8,400 cities and over 700 metropolitan counties reported zero hate crimes to the FBI and to their state officials. These limitations create scenarios where hate crime data may be underreported by victims, law enforcement officers, and agencies.

## Motivation and Theoretical Ecology of Nativism in the Form of Hate Crimes

A vast body of scholarship indicates that hate crimes are a manifestation of a multifaceted behavioral response to out-group threats resulting in criminal activity. Over the past decade and a half, the number of hate crimes has remained constant throughout the United States. Data from the FBI indicates that in 2000 there were 9,096 single-bias hate crimes committed against various racial and ethnic groups, religious organizations, people of various sexual orientations, and individuals with disabilities; by 2015, the number of hate crimes dropped by 31 percent to 6,837.[18] While the overall number of hate crimes decreased for most major groups, crimes against vulnerable populations increased. Vulnerable populations include the homeless, indigent, mentally ill, disabled persons, minorities, children, adolescents, and the elderly.[19] From 2000 to 2015, hate crimes against Muslims increased by 736 percent, hate crimes against Native Americans/Alaskan Natives increased by 113 percent, and hate crimes against individuals with physical and mental disabilities increased by 160 percent and 136 percent.[20]

Of course, not all hate crimes can be attributed to hostile political rhetoric or the divisive political landscape. However, we must consider the role hostile political rhetoric has on legitimizing negative attitudes and stereotypes held by certain groups. Gordon W. Allport, in his seminal book *The Nature of Prejudice*, puts forth the theory that stereotypes are favorable or unfavorable exaggerated beliefs that function to justify and rationalize certain conduct.[21] He goes on to state that a stereotype functions as a "justificatory device" for accepting or rejecting a group; it serves as a superficial screening device.[22] More recent research indicates that stereotypes are contextually based and not necessarily exaggerations or oversimplifications.[23] Stereotypes can be unintentional emotional responses that highlight genuine group differences.[24]

Allport's stereotype theory was inadvertently tested in the 2016 presidential election by Donald Trump, then the Republican presidential nominee. As part of a regular campaign event, Mr. Trump gave a speech in Phoenix, Arizona, on illegal immigration. Mr. Trump painted a picture of Mexican immigrants as criminal aliens freely roaming the streets, doing whatever they wanted and engaging in criminal activity in U.S. communities.[25] In response, three prominent members of white supremacist groups praised the speech and posted comments on Twitter. David Duke, former grand master of the Ku Klux Klan and former Louisiana state representative, tweeted the following: "Excellent speech by Donald Trump tonight. Deport criminal aliens, end catch and release, enforce immigration laws & America First."[26] Richard Spencer, president of a white nationalist think tank, National Policy Institute, tweeted "Diplomacy in the Morning. Nationalism in the evening. #Trump is back in a big way."[27] Jared Taylor, editor of American Renaissance, a white nationalist website, tweeted "#TrumpAZ Hell of a speech. Almost perfect. Logical, deeply felt, and powerfully delivered. Now watch how the media twists it."[28]

On the surface, Mr. Trump's comments on immigration may seem innocuous, but the underlying sweeping categorization of all Mexicans as either criminals or illegally in the United States creates an atmosphere where negative predisposed attitudes about certain groups are legitimized on a global scale. Stereotyping individuals from Mexico is an effortless way to justify the rejection of an ethnic group. The magnification of minority groups as undesirable and a threat makes them "ideal targets since they are visible, available, and vulnerable."[29] Some people who dislike individuals of Mexican descent or immigrants accept the stereotype that justifies their dislike for the group regardless if the stereotype is accurate.[30] Recall from Chapter 1 the father-in-law who purposely "teases" his Puerto Rican friend by calling him a Mexican and saying, "I just laugh and say that he just had to swim farther to get here." Furthermore, research indicates that political attitudes regarding immigration are influenced by "situational triggers" and predisposed biases.[31] In this case, individuals associated with white supremacist groups celebrated Mr. Trump's framing of immigrants as criminals. Political rhetoric that validates unfavorable exaggerated beliefs resonates with those individuals who feel threatened by an out-group. The sense of a perpetuated threat to one's beliefs and practices results in individuals rationalizing their destructive actions as legitimate.[32]

How groups are framed by political rhetoric is an important area to examine. What has occurred since the 2016 presidential election is an increase in hate groups and hate crimes across the country. Negative behavior against minorities is not isolated to adult behavior. The rate of incidents involving adolescents in middle school and high school engaging in hate speech and behavior has increased, forcing school districts to enact policies against the use of racial slurs and negative racial behavior. As in the past, nativism has once again permeated across income, education, and religious levels, manifesting into hate crimes.

## The Social Constructs of Hate Crimes

As demographics in the United States continue to change, blacks, Hispanics, and Asians are set to comprise 51 percent of the total population by 2065.[33] Because of changing demographics, the United States has become more racially and ethnically diverse when compared to any other point in history. Political rhetoric regarding the racial and ethnic diversification of the United States has often been met with nativism and xenophobia. *Nativism* is preserving and or protecting the cultural values of native-born citizens from immigrant influence. Nativism is the fear that immigrants will corrupt existing social mores, traditions, values, religion, class, and culture. The United States has a long history of nativism. Irish, Germans, Italians, Catholics, Chinese, Japanese, Native Americans and other groups have all been targets of nativist rhetoric and actions. The experience of each group is contextual depending on the size of the immigrant group, their economic status, and settling patterns (i.e., rural or suburban community). Similarly, xenophobia is the visceral dislike of foreigners. *Xenophobia* is based on fear of individuals from foreign countries. Xenophobia is tied to nationalism and ethnocentrism and includes a fear of multiculturalism.

In 2007, on *Meet the Press*, a weekly Sunday news program, Pat Buchanan, the Reform Party candidate for U.S. president and former White House speech writer for the Nixon administration and communications director for Ronald Reagan, exchanged views with Congressman Luis Gutiérrez (D-IL) on immigration. Buchanan pointed to "illegal immigration from Mexico as an invasion of criminal felons, child molesters, drunk drivers, rapists and robbers."[34]

Buchanan's political rhetoric construed Mexican immigrants negatively for political gain. Since undocumented immigrants have very little political power, as a group they are political scapegoats for social and economic issues.[35] In addition, negative political rhetoric can compel some citizens to mobilize for or against a candidate based on anger on the issue of immigration.[36] Nativism and xenophobia are rooted in fear; thus, the goal becomes preserving and protecting existing cultural values generally held by the dominant group in a community. How these fears are framed will determine how they manifest into actions. Historically, white elites have dominated the construction of and transmission of which groups belong in the United States. Initiatives such as the Burlingame-Seward Treaty of 1868 and the Bracero Program, juxtaposed against the Chinese Exclusion Act and Operation Wetback, illustrate the complexity and contradictory nature of nativism and xenophobia that results in feelings of perceived threats by outside groups.

Political rhetoric that appeals to emotions of fear and anger and accentuates the differences between groups is effective in creating a polarizing environment of "us against them." The Southern Poverty Law Center estimates that the number of hate groups has increased from 457 in 1999 to 917 in 2016.[37] Additionally, there were a total of 130 Ku Klux Klan groups in 2016 and 193 total Black Separatist groups in 2015.[38] Much of the growth in hate groups can be attributed to the continued growth in the Latino population and changing demographics coupled with negative political rhetoric by political elites.

## Group Threat Theory

As stated in Chapter 1, hate crimes are a manifestation of a complex behavioral response to out-groups, often resulting in unlawful actions. Furthermore, because citizens have cognitive biases that may result in emotions placing a disproportionate weight on an issue,[39] negative political rhetoric taps into the fear and anger that citizens feel about certain racial and ethnic groups. Social science and psychology intellectuals present several theory-based explanations of intergroup hostility when analyzing racial and ethnic conflicts. Group threat theory proposes that hostility and discrimination are a response by dominant groups to perceived threats by inferior groups, since dominant groups view the encroachment of inferior groups as a destabilizing factor to social order.[40] Two key factors undergird group theory. First, inferior groups (out-groups) pose a threat to dominant groups (in-groups) by competing for scarce resources such as employment opportunities and housing.[41] Second, members who strongly identify with the dominant group will attempt to protect group norms (e.g., language, cultural norms) by encouraging negative attitudes toward inferior groups that violate dominant norms.[42] Group threat theory maintains that as the size of the inferior group increases, racial dislike from dominant groups also increases.[43] Fundamentally, prejudice is a response from the dominant group when they feel they may be under threat by members of a subordinate group.[44]

The dominant group's goal is to preserve shared community characteristics and a common American identity. Samuel Huntington, in his essay "The Hispanic Challenge," reveals his own social and defensive idiosyncrasies by stating that immigrants predominantly from Mexico and Latin America do not assimilate to American principles and morals, eroding the Anglo-Protestant culture and American political values. Huntington maintains that the most serious threat and challenge to America's traditional values comes from the continued immigration from Latin America and Mexico, as well as the fertility rates Latino immigrants have when compared to African Americans and white Americans.[45] Huntington underscores the theoretical assumptions of group threat theory by denouncing immigration and lack of assimilation by Hispanic populations. As Ted Brader, Nicholas A. Valentino, and Elizabeth Suhay contend, the growth of diverse ethnic and racial groups serves as a cue to native-born citizens: "Group cues trigger emotions, and these emotions drive opposition."[46] These negative feelings equate to defensive attitudes toward Hispanics, attitudes that can culminate in increased rates of hate crimes against Hispanics.

## Prejudice Model

The prejudice model contends that as part of the human psyche, individuals hold positive and negative attitudes about others and that humans naturally hold prejudicial attitudes toward others.[47] More significant is the idea that attitudes, positive or negative, are learned through social and cultural experiences and are dependent on flawed and obstinate beliefs and generalizations about others.[48] In the United States, these beliefs and generalizations have had negative implications for various racial and ethnic groups.[49] Since relations between racial and ethnic groups are marked by spatial separation, negative attitudes come to fruition via ethnocentrism, the lack of out-group interaction, and by holding generalized views about certain groups.[50] From a societal perspective, negative attitudes and stereotypes based on erroneous beliefs are learned attitudes that result in racial conflict.[51]

Take for example, the New Black Panther Party (NBPP), a black antiwhite and anti-Semitic separatist group whose mission is to unite black people. Under the facade of civil rights activism, the NBPP has pushed forward the idea that blacks should have their own nation and that Jews are responsible for slavery. In 2009, in a National Geographic documentary interview, the leader of the NBPP's Philadelphia charter, King Samir Shabazz, makes the following comments in regard to whites: "I hate white people. All of them. Every last iota of a cracker. . . You want freedom? You going to have to kill some crackers! You going to have to kill some of their babies."[52] Although the NBPP is not a political organization, they are a community organization with enormous influence, and they are responsible for instigating verbal and non-verbal microaggressions against other groups.

In another example of stereotypes based on erroneous beliefs, at a roast for controversial Maricopa County Sheriff Joe Arpaio in 2014, Arizona state representative John Kavanagh repeatedly made jokes about Hispanics, saying "going out with Sheriff Joe is always an adventure because usually when we walk into a restaurant most of the wait staff and cooks dive out the back window, and when they don't I never know what the hell is in my food. Here's a great one, get 'em, sic 'em." Representative Kavanagh continued his roast by closing with the following remarks (referring to the federal investigation of Arpaio for contempt of court charges stemming from continued racial profiling against Latinos):

> Just to show you how unreasonable the federal monitor is [they're demanding that] when Sheriff Joe sends his new deputies to the academy, he will no longer just train them to do the Miranda warning in Spanish, he will have to teach it in English too. . . . the sign over the booking intake door in the jail will have to have "welcome" and just not "bienvenido" . . . And with that, adios.[53]

In the example above, Representative Kavanagh holds negative and prejudicial attitudes about Latinos. His negative attitude about Latinos was a learned process reinforced through social and cultural experiences. At the roast, Mr. Kavanagh received repeated applause and laughter from the audience over his denigrating remarks about Latinos. This positive reception served as encouragement to continue with his off-color jokes.

## Realistic Group Conflict Theory

Realistic group conflict theory suggests that prejudice and discrimination are a result of competition between groups for limited resources.[54] Scholars of realistic group conflict maintain that intergroup conflict increases when competition for scarce resources is based on the perception that one group may yield higher benefits from the resource than the competing group.[55] The greater the out-group threat, the higher the hostility toward the perceived threat.[56] However, when competing groups cooperate with each other, this yields positive results, but negative intergroup competition or the lack of cooperation yields negative attitudes and actions.[57] Intergroup conflicts occur when in-groups identify more closely with other similar social units; these units (or groups) share similar language and communication characteristics, creating an in-group–out-group dichotomy.[58]

For instance, immigrant groups to the United States have faced realistic group conflict in various forms. From 1840 to 1914, European immigrants from Ireland, Germany, and Southern and Eastern Europe were targets of prejudice and discrimination. Immigrants from Europe were fleeing political and religious persecution or escaping famine, while others came to the United States in search of economic opportunities. Initially, most of these immigrant groups were welcomed into society for their cheap labor. However, the growing influx of immigrants created competition for scarce resources that native populations had dominated. Because European immigrants were seen as a threat, native citizens projected hostility toward immigrant groups (outgroups). In addition, perceptions of shifting political power are not a new phenomenon among native-born citizens. Societal opposition toward immigrants has occurred throughout history. One example is the American Party, also known as the "Know-Nothing Party," in Ohio from the mid-1840s to the late 1850s. The Know-Nothing Party was composed of white Protestant working-class men who opposed immigration, Catholics, and Jews. The Know-Nothings feared that immigrants would create competition for scarce jobs, and they believed immigrants belonging to the Catholic Church would pledge their allegiance to the pope, a foreign power, and not the United States.[59]

## Defended Neighborhood Theory

Defended neighborhood theory proposes that at the local neighborhood level, intergroup violence occurs when ethnic integration threatens ethnically homogenous neighborhoods.[60] In its original conceptualization, ethnically homogenous neighborhoods that share similar social characteristics react negatively and defensively when racial and ethnic demographics threaten the cohesion of an established community.[61] When white majority communities perceive a threat to their shared characteristics and/or common identity, they respond by committing racially motivated crimes against the in-migration of ethnic groups.[62]

Historian Kevin M. Kruse succinctly illustrates how powerful defended neighborhood theory can be in his account of white flight in Atlanta, Georgia, in the 1960s. Kruse tells the story of how Southern cities faced the challenges of the civil rights era. Atlanta had successfully desegregated public schools, which captured the attention of the president of the United States, admirers across the country, and the press.[63] One year after all the national attention and accolades, trouble surfaced in a quiet, white, middle-income neighborhood named Peyton Forest.[64] Residents were predominantly white and had noticed an increase in blacks purchasing homes in and around "their" community. As a result of the increase in blacks leaving the inner city and relocating to customarily white neighborhoods, newly elected mayor Ivan Allen Jr. approved city construction of barricades blocking off access to Peyton Forest and the surrounding area. The barriers were significant because they were erected on the fault line that separated black and white neighborhoods in Atlanta. There was an immediate uproar to the barricades by civil rights activists, but Peyton Forest residents welcomed the barriers in hopes of keeping blacks out of their neighborhoods. Several prominent white homeowners threatened to sell their homes, while others expressed concern that the entire city of Atlanta would be overrun by blacks. In the end, blacks continued to purchase homes in the Peyton Forest area, and whites sold their homes and relocated to other areas. In this example, Kruse captures the visceral reaction whites had to blacks moving into their community. In this case, the essence of defended neighborhood theory is preserving white homogeneity against racial integration. The negative reaction to integration by whites in Peyton Forest is not an isolated case that is applicable to whites only. The same negative reaction occurs when African Americans purchase homes or move to predominantly Latino neighborhoods; when Latinos move to predominantly white and African American neighborhoods; and more recently, when Muslims move to predominantly white, African American, and/or Latino neighborhoods. Racially and ethnically homogenous neighborhoods respond negatively to the encroachment of disparate ethnic groups.

## American Groups as Microaggression Targets

Preamble to the Declaration of Independence:

We hold these truths to be self-evident, that all men are created equal, that they are endowed by their Creator with certain unalienable Rights, that among these are Life, Liberty, and the pursuit of Happiness.

The Preamble to the U.S. Constitution:

We the people of the United States, in order to form a more perfect union, establish justice, insure domestic tranquility, provide for the common defense, promote the general welfare, and secure the blessings of liberty to ourselves and our posterity, do ordain and establish this Constitution for the United States of America.

The Declaration of Independence and the U.S. Constitution, two of America's founding documents, were written to explain why the colonists were seeking independence from Great Britain and to express ideals of freedom that rest upon citizens themselves. The caveat to America's founding documents was that at the time they excluded most white men and women, and slaves and Native Americans were characterized as inferior or subhuman.[65] At the inception of America's founding, these groups were not entitled to equality, unalienable rights, justice, tranquility, or the promotion of general welfare. This form of political rhetoric and thought were widely held beliefs by white Europeans of this era; these microaggressive declarative beliefs regarding outside groups were interwoven into numerous powerful U.S. documents, setting the stage for the founding of American ideals.

The intent here is not to disparage the process in which the United States was founded, but to point out that throughout history certain groups integral to the creation and success of America were explicitly omitted from the rights and protections bestowed on others. Since the founding of America these groups have contended with two central themes. The first is that through political institutions certain groups have been victims of microaggressive behavior. These institutions include, but are not limited to, the various branches of government, the education system, and legislation. Structurally, institutions function at various microaggressive degrees within an individual's lifespan. Microaggressions are not static and have long-lasting negative effects. The second is that these same groups have been vilified by political elite rhetoric. The vilification process is not limited to race and ethnicity, but also includes gender, religion, citizenship status, and patriotism. To sufficiently understand how political microaggressions affect the disenfranchisement of certain groups, the aim here is to provide a holistic perspective on how powerful and damaging political microaggressions are at stereotyping and demeaning an individual or an entire group.[66]

## African Americans

In two hundred years of slavery, an estimated 10 to 60 million black Africans were either enslaved or died during transport on slave ships to the United States.[67] Naomi Mandel describes the vast range in the estimated number of slaves in the following way:

> There is, however, a significant difference between those who never made it into slavery, on the one hand, and those who died in Africa and on slave ships in addition to the victims of slavery itself, on the other. So drastic a revision of the figure's referent within so short a space of time itself attests to the significant absence of adequate documentation of the atrocities perpetrated by slaveholders, slave traders, and the institution of American slavery.

Political and institutional systems created an environment where slavery was considered the norm.[68] For all intents and purposes, many of the Founding Fathers who promoted ideals of liberty and justice were not opposed to the idea of a "permanent slave state" or the genocide of Native Americans.[69] In that era, numerous U.S. presidents and Founding Fathers (e.g., Thomas Paine, William Penn, Benjamin Franklin, Thomas Jefferson, George Washington, and others) at one point in time were enslavers of human beings.[70] These prominent and revered political figures were responsible for setting in motion the institution of slavery in the United States. Because the idea of slavery was deeply ingrained, slaves were considered an economic necessity and dehumanized, which had an immense economic and social effect[71] on how African Americans were and are viewed in the modern era. Fundamentally, the institution of slavery is one of many egregious microaggressions that still frames how African Americans are viewed. As such, slavery has been sufficiently examined by many intellectuals and does not require an extended discussion.[72] Instead, here I attempt to shed light on how political discourse and policies manifest into microaggressions that have negative effects on African Americans.

After the Civil War in 1865, the Reconstruction era set into motion events that should have guaranteed former slaves basic institutional and constitutional rights. The era marked the federal government's attempt at instituting requirements for Confederate Southern slave states to reenter the Union. The U.S. Constitution was amended to abolish slavery, grant citizenship status to individuals born or naturalized in the United States, and to grant voting rights to African American men (the Thirteenth, Fourteenth, and Fifteenth Amendments of the U.S. Constitution). While these rights should have to some extent "evened the playing field" for African Americans, most Southern states ignored the federal government's mandates and created their own Jim Crow laws to continue the subjugation of and microaggressive behavior against African Americans.

In *Plessy v. Ferguson*, the U.S. Supreme Court upheld de jure segregation or legal racial segregation. The case established the separate but equal doctrine, which mandated racially separate accommodations on buses, schools, theaters, restaurants, and many other places. Racial inequality was enforced through signs posted with "No Niggers Welcomed Here"[73] and "Colored served in the back." As William Eskridge notes, with the *Plessy* ruling the court did nothing to protect people of color from race-based prejudicial classifications.[74] The opinion by the highest legal institution in the United States continued to promote microaggressive policies that negatively affected people of color. De facto segregation was not mandated by law, but racial segregation led to the isolation of African Americans in terms of housing and education, creating highly segregated communities.[75] Although not required by law, the normalization of de facto segregation also resulted in microaggressive race-based classifications.

In what seemed to be a positive move of recognizing the unequal guarantees of liberty and justice to African Americans, in *Brown v. Board of Education* (1954), the U.S. Supreme Court ruled that separate but equal doctrine regarding children attending public schools violated the Equal Protection Clause of the Fourteenth Amendment, and the court struck down de jure racial segregation.[76] With the ruling that separate but equal violated the Equal Protection Clause, whites resorted to Jim Crow laws to keep African Americans subservient. Jim Crow laws were racist, oppressive, anti–African American segregationist laws. Local and state governments, communities, the education system, and the judicial system all supported Jim Crow laws, continuing the oppression of African Americans and other racial minorities. This led to the continued brutal beatings and lynchings by whites if African Americans resisted subjugation.[77]

In a classic example of political speech as a weapon, President Dwight D. Eisenhower, often characterized as a strong military leader and a five-star general in the Army, publicly supported the civil rights movement but in private expressed his concern over the *Brown* ruling to Supreme Court Chief Justice Earl Warren.[78] Eisenhower commented that he could sympathize with Southerners' concern over integration "to see their sweet little girls required to sit in a school alongside some big black buck."[79] Eisenhower used a racial slur to depict African American men, an intentional comment meant to communicate a derogatory and negative insult—a classic microaggression.

Research by legal historian and constitutional law scholar Michael Klarman on the relationship between civil rights, race relations, and rulings by the Supreme Court examines the direct and inadvertent consequences of some of the court's civil rights rulings and the persistent racial inequality in the United States.[80] He found that institutional Jim Crow laws were symbolic:

> Much of Jim Crow was concerned with symbolism, including rules of sidewalk etiquette, refusals to extend courtesy titles to blacks, and expectations of black submissiveness. . . . After black disenfranchisement, politicians had little incentive to resist any segregationist proposal. Just as politicians today compete to demonstrate toughness on crime, candidates under Jim Crow had to constantly affirm their commitment to white supremacy.[81]

In an illustration of how framing supports the idea that whites sit at a higher hierarchical level than other groups, in November 2016 Mayor Beverly Whaling of Clay, West Virginia, temporarily resigned from her position after posting support for denigrating remarks made about then-current first lady Michelle Obama. The events on Facebook developed quickly: Pamela Ramsey, the Clay County development director, posted the following comment: "It will be refreshing to have a classy, beautiful, dignified First Lady in the White House. I'm tired of seeing a Ape in heels." Beverly Whaling, the Clay mayor, responded on Facebook: "Just made my day Pam."[82]

Another example of how white framing reinforces the notion that whites sit at a higher hierarchical level is from former U.S. senator Robert Byrd (D-WV). Byrd had a long and distinguished career in the Senate and openly discussed the shame he felt over his membership in the Ku Klux Klan. However, prior to remorsefulness and apologizing for being a Klan member and an oppressor of civil rights, Byrd, in a letter to Senator Theodore Bilboa, a segregationist from Mississippi, wrote: "I shall never fight in the armed forces with a negro by my side. . . . Rather I should die a thousand times, and see Old Glory trampled in the dirt never to rise again, than to see this beloved land of ours become degraded by race mongrels, a throwback to the blackest specimen from the wilds."[83]

The disparaging comments from public officials regarding the First Lady of the United States overshadow Michelle Obama's achievements of being an Ivy League (Princeton and Harvard Law School) graduate, attorney, a mother, assistant commissioner of planning and development in Chicago, founding executive director of Chicago's chapter of Public Allies, and the first African American First Lady.[84] Instead, the framing of the Facebook posts depicts an accomplished individual as less than human. Byrd's comments in his letter to a segregationist are similar to Pamela Ramsey's, in which blacks are framed as less than human. The prejudice model discussed earlier in this chapter contends that positive or negative attitudes are learned through socialization and cultural experiences, and are often based on flawed beliefs and generalizations about others.[85] These beliefs and generalizations have a negative impact on various racial and ethnic groups.[86] Political rhetoric that appeals to emotions and draws attention to differences between individuals is effective in creating a polarizing environment of "us against them." Negative political rhetoric, particularly microaggressions, matter in politics because this rhetoric is effective at providing a platform in which our elected representatives and regular American citizens feel comfortable openly discriminating against certain people and groups.

Recall from Chapter 1 that microassaults are a form of microaggressions. Microassaults are the equivalent of old-fashioned racism. The online exchange between Clay County development director Pamela Ramsey and Beverly Whaling, the Clay city mayor, illustrates how public officials at all levels of government use political microaggressions as a weapon to deliberately ostracize a person. Political institutions have framed how people view and interact with African Americans. Microaggressions toward people of color were and continue to be institutionalized by public officials at all levels of government, which when framed in this manner normalizes microaggressive behavior.

## Asian Americans

U.S. Census 2015 data indicates that Asians are projected to be the second fastest-growing racial group in the United States by 2060. As of 2014, the Asian-alone population accounted for 20 million,[87] or 5.4 percent, of the total U.S. population.[88] By 2060, Asians are projected to account for 22 million, or 9.3 percent, of the total U.S. population.[89] Although population projections continue to increase for Asians, the group's presence in the United States has been largely understated. In the 1800s, as the United States positioned itself to expand its economic trade with Asia, it was able to negotiate the Burlingame-Seward Treaty with China. As part of the agreement, Chinese immigrants and laborers would be allowed to freely travel to the United States on the same terms as European immigrants, and the treaty provided reciprocal protection to Chinese and U.S. citizens traveling and living abroad.[90] In return, the United States assured itself of cheap immigrant labor and access to trading opportunities in Asian markets.

Since the 1860s, Chinese immigrants have made a significant economic impact to the United States. Because of the California Gold Rush and the ability of Chinese immigrants to travel to the United States, Chinese immigrants began arriving in the United States in large numbers. In the mid-1860s, California became one of two states to begin construction on the transcontinental railroad that would extend over two thousand miles of rugged terrain. As in most cases when the United States has needed cheap labor, it "opened the immigrant gate" to pursue economic feasibility. Irish, German, and especially Chinese immigrants worked in grueling and dangerous conditions to lay the tracks for the transcontinental railroad. The Central Pacific Railroad Company brought thousands of Chinese laborers to the United States to build the western side of the transcontinental railroad.[91] (Soon afterward, American businesses that supported the transcontinental railroad began to use a contract labor system, which allowed employers to contract labor and/or coolies at wages below market rates to recruit cheaper and faster labor from China.[92]) With the demand to complete the transcontinental railroad, the Chinese became the major group in the construction of the railroad.

However, the inundation of Chinese laborers coupled with the large influx of German and Irish already in the United States created an overabundance of immigrant labor, leading to a movement toward immigration restrictions. Chinese immigrants exploited for their cheap labor soon became racial targets. In 1866, a contentious debate between U.S. House of Representatives William Higby of California and William Niblack of Indiana deliberated the proposal of the Fourteenth Amendment to the Constitution. In this exchange, microaggressive verbal insults concerning Chinese immigrants were espoused.

Niblack questioned Higby, an advocate of the adoption of the amendment, on the impact to Californian Chinese immigrants if the Fourteenth Amendment were to be adopted. Higby was quoted as saying:

> the Chinese are nothing but a pagan race. They are an enigma to me, although I have lived among them for fifteen years. You cannot make good citizens of them; they do not learn the language of the country. . . . They buy and sell their women like cattle, and the trade is mostly for the purpose of prostitution. You cannot make citizens of them.[93]

One of several significant political microaggressions committed against Asians was the adoption of the Chinese Exclusion Act of 1882, enacted by Congress instead of repealing the Burlingame-Seward Treaty. The Chinese Exclusion Act was the first immigration law specifically restricting the flow of immigrants; some of the key provisions halted Chinese immigration for a period of 10 years, barred Chinese immigrants from naturalization, and allowed illegal Chinese immigrants to be deported.[94] Later, through the Geary Act of 1892, the exclusionary law against Chinese was extended for an additional 10 years; it took 60 years to finally repeal the act in 1943.

More recently, in the 2016 presidential election, candidates running for the Republican nomination began verbally sparring over the term *anchor baby*. The term is considered derogatory and is typically used when debating immigration issues; it refers to a baby born in the United States to parents who are undocumented. In the 2016 presidential race, Republican candidates used political rhetoric to single out certain racial and ethnic groups. Jeb Bush, former governor of Florida, downplayed his use of the term by shifting the focus from Latinos who are typically associated with the term to Asians. Bush stated the following: "Frankly, it's more related to Asian people coming into our country, having children in that organized effort, taking advantage of a noble concept, which is birthright citizenship. Those babies were involved in a fraud."[95]

In this instance, Bush attempted to deflect for his gaffe of using the term at an earlier stop at the U.S.-Mexico border. Instead, Bush disparaged individuals of Asian ancestry. In an attempt to not scapegoat Latinos, Bush's comments on Asians may seem harmless, but as in the Trump example earlier, the underlying sweeping categorization of all Asians as anchor babies creates an environment where negative characterizations about certain groups are validated on cable television. Recall from Chapter 1 that individuals will self-sort to news that reinforces what they think. Framing Asians as a whole as only interested in birthright citizenship is an easy way to justify the microaggressive behavior of an entire ethnic group. Another significant political microaggression committed against Asians was imprisoning Japanese immigrants in internment camps after the attack on Pearl Harbor. Recall from earlier parts of this chapter that the magnification of minority groups as undesirable and a threat makes them "ideal targets since they are visible, available, and vulnerable."[96]

## Latinos

As outlined in Chapter 2, demographics in the United States continue to change. As of 2016, U.S. births to Latino parents now make up the majority of the Latino population, not immigration.[97] The change in demographics creates conditions where American-born Latinos are at risk of nativism simply based on the issue of immigration. Over the past several decades, data clearly indicates that the estimated number of undocumented immigrants increased to an estimated 11 million, with the estimated totals declining to 10 million between 2010 and 2017,[98] exacerbating xenophobic perceptions. Since 2000, data has consistently shown that at least half of the estimated undocumented immigrants in the United States originate from Mexico or Central and Latin American countries.[99] The way immigration is framed by elected officials and the media leads the general public to conceptualize all Latinos as undocumented immigrants from Mexico or Central America. The immigration of various ethnic groups is not a modern-day contemporary issue, nor is the anti-immigrant rhetoric. Xenophobic attitudes and perceptions have depicted immigrant groups as threats to an American identity legally and socially defined by whiteness.[100]

Political institutions have been the venue for microaggressive behavior, vilifying groups by political elite rhetoric. Much like African Americans and Chinese Americans, the negative racializing framework of Latinos is not a new phenomenon.[101] The framing of Latinos as undocumented with large families, inferior cultures, and unable to speak the English language makes this population an easy target of negative political rhetoric. Long before Donald Trump, the 2016 republican candidate and party nominee, made national headlines with Twitter statements regarding Mexico and Mexicans (". . . .likewise, billions of dollars gets brought into Mexico through the border. We get the killers, drugs, & crime, they get the money!"[102]) Latinos have been targets of microaggressive behavior from various political outlets. Former U.S. president James Polk, who served from 1845 to 1849, was an advocate of Manifest Destiny—the quest for expanding the United States to the west. As part of Polk's rationale to expand into Mexican territory (now Arizona, California, New Mexico, and Texas), he claimed the United States had the right to invade and take land from Mexico and to rule over backward people.[103] Throughout his presidency, Polk remained steadfast to the idea of U.S. expansionism into Mexican territory, ultimately culminating in the Mexican-American War of 1846, which was fought over border disputes. Mexico, on the verge of defeat, agreed to the Treaty of Guadalupe Hidalgo of 1848, ending the Mexican-American War. Some of the provisions of the treaty required Mexico to cede territory to the United States, and it required the United States to pay Mexico $15,000,000 for the newly acquired land. The treaty also allowed Mexicans living in Texas to either become automatic citizens of the United States with all the protections, rights, and privileges as other U.S. citizens, or they could return to Mexican territory.[104]

Institutionally, the expansion into Mexico and the taking of territory is not a new phenomenon. Expansionism occurred with Native American tribes losing their land when European squatters arrived in North America. Because the Treaty of Guadalupe called for the incorporation of Mexican citizens into the union, Senator John C. Calhoun in a speech expressed his concern over allowing a lesser race into the United States:

> I know further, sir, that we have never dreamt of incorporating into our Union any but the Caucasian race—the free white race. To incorporate Mexico would be the very first instance of the kind of incorporating an Indian race; for more than half of the Mexicans are Indians, and the other half is composed chiefly of mixed tribes. I protest against such a union as that! Ours, sir, is the Government of a white race. The greatest misfortunes of Spanish America are to be traced to the fatal error of placing these colored races on an equality with the white race.[105]

The history of Latinos in the United States is complex and often met with nativist and xenophobic attitudes from multiple other groups. Negative political rhetoric provides political framing for how individuals view and interact with Latinos. To illustrate the point of how negative political rhetoric impacts Latinos, consider that Governor Jan Brewer (R-AZ), in an interview on Fox News, compared illegal immigration to terrorist attacks. In reference to the specifics in Arizona, Brewer stated: "We reap all the criminal activities, kidnappings, the drugs, the cartels, the decimation of our country side. . . . We will not tolerate illegal immigration bringing with it . . . the implications of crime and terrorism into our state."[106] Commentary about immigration may seem rational, but the classification of all illegal immigrants as criminals or terrorists creates an atmosphere where negative predisposed attitudes about immigrants are legitimized by public officials. Recall from Chapter 2 that half of all undocumented immigrants are from Mexico and Central and Latin America, putting a spotlight on all Latinos regardless of their citizenship status.

Following the 2016 U.S. presidential campaign, in which building a border wall between the United States and Mexico received praise from supporters, the Southern Poverty Law Center found that 32 percent of hate crimes were motivated by anti-immigrant sentiment.[107] In Punta Gorda, Florida, an argument between a Hispanic family and a woman who nearly drove through a crosswalk escalated when she told them they "should all be deported." In Dallas, Texas, an older white man walked by a Hispanic man and, unprovoked, yelled, "Go back to Mexico!" In Tuscola County, Michigan, a Latino family was shocked to find a wall of boxes scrawled with "Trump," "Take America Back," and "Mexicans suck." In Colorado Springs, Colorado, 8th grade students told Latino students on the school bus, "Not only should Trump build a wall, but it should be electrocuted [*sic*] and Mexicans should have to wear shock collars."[108]

Structurally, institutions have framed how Latinos are viewed within society. Latinos have been characterized as "backward" individuals that are racially and ethnically inferior to whites and as undocumented immigrants regardless of their longstanding history as U.S. citizens. Microaggressions in the form of speeches have long-lasting negative effects on the recipient of the political attack, but not those who agree with the rhetoric. Today, as in the past, political rhetoric can frame policy issues, individuals, and groups in positive or negative undertones. Political framing provides a heuristic shortcut for how people view and interact with each other.

## Muslims

On September 11, 2001, the United States was attacked by 19 Islamic extremists who hijacked four planes. At 8:46 a.m. a plane crashed into the North Tower of the World Trade Center. At 9:03 a.m. a second plane crashed into the South Tower of the World Trade Center. Thirty-five minutes later, at 9:37 a.m., a third plane crashed into the Pentagon, and at 10:03 a.m. a fourth plane crashed in Somerset County, Pennsylvania.[109] More than 2,600 people died at the World Trade Center; 125 died at the Pentagon; 256 died on the four planes. The death toll surpassed that at Pearl Harbor in December 1941.[110]

After the 9/11 attacks anti-Muslim hate crimes increased from 28 in 2000 to 481 incidents in 2001.[111] Sixteen years after the terrorist attacks, recent survey research indicates that 49 percent of American adults think at least some Muslims in the United States are anti-American, while 11 percent think most or all Muslims are anti-American.[112] These inaccurate views about Muslims are reinforced by public officials. The institutional framing that all Muslims are terrorists creates conditions ripe for microaggressions against this population. In 2015, Donald Trump entered the U.S. presidential campaign calling for a complete and total shutdown of Muslims entering the country and suggested a registry for Muslims already in the United States.[113] The FBI reported that since Trump's entry into politics hate crimes against Muslims have increased by 67 percent and crimes against Muslims have been the highest since 2001, right after 9/11.[114]

The microaggressive political rhetoric during the 2016 U.S. presidential elections has had a negative impact on Muslims in the United States. As of

2017, political speech continues to be used as a weapon to characterize all Muslims as the antithesis of American values. Institutionally, on January 27, 2017, as a way to reinforce the negative connotations associated with Muslims, Mr. Trump signed Executive Order 13769 (Protecting the Nation from Foreign Terrorist Entry into the United States),[115] banning immigration from seven Muslim countries. On September 14, 2016, Joseph Schreiber, a Port St. Lucie, Florida, resident, set fire to the Islamic Center of Fort Pierce where Pulse nightclub shooter Omar Mateen worshiped. Authorities received several tips that led to Mr. Schreiber being a prime suspect for the fire. As part of the investigation, authorities searched Mr. Schreiber's social media accounts and found several anti-Islamic posts and references to 9/11.[116] For example, a July 12 post on Mr. Schreiber's Facebook page stated:

> IF AMERICA truly wants peace and safety and pursuit of happiness they should consider all forms of ISLAM as radical. The truth is that there is no such thing as radical ISLAMIC extremism. . . . ALL ISLAM IS RADICAL.[117]

Although there may be numerous underlying reasons as to why Mr. Schreiber set fire to an Islamic mosque, his actions underscore the framing of Muslims as radical terrorists. When political elites engage in framing a group as inferior to dominant values and concerns, it raises the number of opportunities for microaggressions against a population.

## Conclusion

Microassaults are a variation of microaggressions, which are often conscious, intentional, biased beliefs or attitudes expressed primarily by a violent verbal or nonverbal attack meant to hurt a marginalized person or group. A microassault is "old-fashioned racism," where an action is conscious and deliberate. This chapter examined nativist and xenophobic attitudes as a form of microaggressions against African Americans, Asians, Latinos, and Muslims and offered several complex theories on behavioral responses to out-groups often resulting in unlawful actions. This chapter examined the long history of nativism and xenophobia in the United States. Nativism is the fear that out-groups (particularly immigrants) will corrupt existing social mores, traditions, values, religion, class, and culture. Xenophobia is based on fear of individuals from foreign countries and is tied to nationalism and ethnocentrism, which includes a fear of multiculturalism.

In addition, several behavioral response theories were examined, each providing a framework for how individuals view policy issues and the ways individuals and groups respond to each other that result in the use of microaggressions. Group threat theory proposes that hostility and discrimination are a response by dominant groups to perceived threats by inferior groups. In this case, dominant groups view the encroachment of inferior groups as a destabilizing factor to social order, because inferior groups pose a threat by competing for scarce resources (e.g., employment and housing). The prejudice model argues that individuals hold positive and negative attitudes about others and that humans naturally hold prejudicial attitudes. It is the idea that attitudes, positive or negative, are learned through social and cultural experiences and are dependent on flawed beliefs and generalizations about others. Realistic group conflict theory suggests that prejudice and discrimination are a result of competition between groups for limited resources, resulting in increased intergroup conflict. The last of the behavioral response theories examined was defended neighborhood theory. This theory suggests that ethnically homogenous neighborhoods that share similar social characteristics react negatively and defensively when racial and ethnic demographics threaten the cohesion of an established community. Essentially, as long as all the neighbors look alike, there is some form of cohesion, but when the racial and ethnic make-up of a neighborhood begins to change, the original neighbors begin to feel threatened. These behavioral response theories are used to frame how groups of people interact with each other and/or are at odds with each other. More important, these theories can be linked to the use of microaggressions not only by elected officials but also by the general population.

Political rhetoric by public officials often frames how individuals interact and respond to each other. Consider the vignette that will be discussed in Chapter 5, where outside of a Starbucks a white woman attacked a woman wearing a hijab. The attacker yelled "Muslim piece of trash" and indicated she was voting for Trump and hoped he would send "all of you terrorist Muslims out of this country."[118] In this case, because of the rhetoric used in the 2016 presidential election, the white woman displayed several of the behavioral response theories based on how Trump negatively framed Muslims throughout the campaign. Of course, not all criminal activity can be attributed to hostile political rhetoric or the divisive political landscape. But, we must consider that when elected officials use their platforms to denigrate groups, in some cases it does legitimize negative attitudes and stereotypes held by other groups. Hostile political rhetoric opens the door and provides a platform for those individuals or groups that already hold negative attitudes and stereotypes about other groups. Microaggressions espoused from the highest levels of leadership give a voice to individuals and/or groups that already have an inclination to act upon rhetoric that validates their preconceived attitudes. This is why negative political rhetoric in the form of microaggressions matters in U.S. politics. Microaggressions create an environment where elected officials and members of a community openly disparage and discriminate against certain individuals and groups, which results in biased public policies.

# The Realization That Times Are Changing

On April 21, 2016, in Washington, DC, police said a woman wearing a hijab was approached outside of a Starbucks by a white woman shouting "Muslim piece of trash." The white woman walked away briefly, but returned to pour an unknown liquid on the woman's head. The Council on American Islamic Relations stated that the suspect had indicated she was voting for Trump and hoped he would send "all of you terrorist Muslims out of this country."[1]

As discussed in Chapter 2, demographics are changing in the United States. Changing demographics mean changes in race and ethnicity, cultures, religions, and attitudes about shifting demographics. African Americans, Asian Americans, and Latinos currently comprise a larger share of the U.S. population than they have in any other period in history. The United States is more ethnically and racially diverse, resulting in a more multicultural and multilingual population. Even though ethnic and racial diversification continues to increase, as of 2014, non-Hispanic whites still comprised the largest share of the U.S. population at slightly over 50 percent.[2] Despite this, by the year 2060, population projections will shift, and the share of non-Hispanic whites will fall to less than 50 percent of the overall U.S. population.[3] Changing demographics suggest that the electorate is also changing, which in turn affects the institutions responsible for creating public policy at the local, state, and national level. U.S.-born Hispanic children (i.e., millennials) currently make up the largest share of eligible voters, and they are expected to maintain that momentum in the foreseeable future.[4] What does this mean for political microaggressions or microaggressions in general? Recall from Chapter 1 the native

Pakistani physician who was shopping at a local WalMart in West Texas when he and his wife were approached by a white man yelling "Get out of my country, make American great again," and the 2017 shooting death of Srinivas Kuchibhotla, a legally authorized immigrant from India, at a sports bar in Kansas City, Missouri. Before firing his 9 mm semiautomatic handgun, Adam W. Purinton was quoted as shouting "Get out of my country." Can we expect more microaggressions because of changing demographics? Was Samuel Huntington right when in a microassaultive statement he argued that the only American dream was an Anglo-Saxon dream and Mexican Americans could share in the dream only if they dream in English? As I have argued throughout the book, political microaggressions are about how individuals, groups, and organizations are framed by individuals, particularly elected officials with biased views, racist inclinations, and preconceived stereotypes. The claim has also been that many microaggressions are intentional and not unconscious as other research indicates. When the white man yelled at the native Pakistani physician at WalMart and when Adam W. Purinton walked in to a Kansas City bar and discharged his weapon, both were intentional acts brought on by nativist inclinations that result in hate speech and hate crimes. These are prime examples of why negative rhetoric in U.S. politics matters. Hostile rhetoric is effective at creating an environment in which politicians and regular American citizens feel comfortable acting out against certain people and groups.

In the vignette at the beginning of the chapter and in the Pakistani physician and Srinivas Kuchibhotla cases, U.S. political elites and other information outlets have subtly and overtly framed individuals from foreign countries as terrorists regardless of their country of origin, resulting in citizens acting on fears that demographics are changing, exacerbating an "us versus them" climate. Political microaggressions are tools in a much larger political spectrum that are effective in suppressing groups that may not necessarily align with Anglo-Protestant views.[5] Issues such as economic, political, and social equality are part of a larger discussion about the hierarchical status of minorities in America and the extent to which minorities will define future public policies and political debate. Political microaggressions are akin to Pandora's box: while insults and hostile rhetoric allow individuals and political elites to define the political landscape, the effects provide a platform for nativists, extremists, and hate groups to portray certain groups as threatening by insisting that they are only saying what everyone else is thinking or doing what everyone wishes they could do. For example, shouting "Get out of my country, make American great again," can be interpreted as an attempt to maintain Anglo-Protestant practices in language, religion, and politics. Hostility and antipathy toward minorities and foreigners can be seen as upholding American values, mores, and traditions. Microaggressions have become normalized idioms (e.g., "take our country back") where ordinary citizens feel empowered to consciously act on such rhetoric.

The significance of political microaggressions on minorities should not be understated. Political microaggressions directed toward minorities can be understood in two distinct ways: one, they frame economic, political, and social inequality problems by placing the blame on minorities themselves; and, two, they provide shortcuts for individuals to distinguish between "us versus them," which provide a stimulus for acting out against minorities. Because of this framing, political issues such as economic, political, and social inequality may not receive the political attention required to result in change. For example, elected officials have been grappling with issues of inequality for decades; however, the institutionalized response (i.e., from local, state, and federal governments) has been more cuts to programs that directly affect the populations, typically minority groups in need of parity.[6] Individuals framed as not sharing Anglo-Protestant values, whatever those values may be, are not seen as a priority when compared to other political issues regardless of the assurances during campaigns to level the playing field.[7] By targeting minorities with political microaggressions and making it an "us versus them" framework, microaggressions become part of institutional systems that govern the masses. When microaggressions are institutionalized, they have the potential to impede minorities from achieving economic, political, and social stability. And, even when minorities do manage to succeed in one of the three areas, there is speculation that affirmative action or other preference must have been given to an individual or group in order for them to succeed. Recall from Chapter 1 the first-year female graduate student who received stipend funding and was accused by her white male colleague of only receiving funding because she was the "token female and minority" in the group. At a much larger level, one of the most egregious cases of institutional racial microaggressions occurred in 1999. The framing involved Wen Ho Lee, a naturalized U.S. citizen, PhD in mechanical engineering, and scientist at Los Alamos National Laboratory in New Mexico. Lee was falsely accused of engaging in espionage for the Chinese government because of his Chinese ethnicity. In his book *My Country Versus Me*, Lee recalls the untruths, cover-ups, and false information the U.S. government manufactured to falsely accuse him of espionage. While incarcerated Lee had the following realization: "As I sat in jail, I had to conclude that no matter how smart you are, no matter how hard you work, a Chinese person, an Asian person like me, will never be accepted. We always will be foreigners."[8]

Optics and rhetoric emphasized that Lee was a naturalized U.S. citizen from China who had frequent interactions with other Chinese scientists, and that his wife spoke Mandarin. These optics were enough for the federal government to fabricate allegations of espionage against him.[9] Although this may be an extreme case of racist microaggressions, Lee's case was framed as an "us versus them" national issue. Microaggressions can undermine democratic values such as liberty, justice, and equality and override common sense. More important, undermining democratic values not only affects minorities, but its reach also impacts non-Hispanic whites. Regardless of race or ethnicity, microaggressions erode trust and belief in government institutions and the democratic values that most perpetrators of microaggressions claim are important in identifying as American (e.g., the Bill of Rights, the Constitution). The recognition that economic, political, and social stratification affect all races, ethnicities, neighborhoods, families, and friends and that only 1 percent of Americans hold all the wealth in the United States, along with the understanding that political microaggressions are used to create an "us versus them" environment, will erode trust in political elites. Moreover, the erosion of trust and belief in government institutions will continue until citizens become conscious that political elites deflect and obfuscate the needs of the very people they indirectly microaggress.

This chapter examines changing demographics and the idea that regardless of race, ethnicity, gender, religion, class, or geographic location, individuals continue to identify as American. While majority-minority populations might be transitioning from one to another, individual ideals of what it means to be an American are not clear cut and democratic values continue to hold strong regardless of political rhetoric infused with microaggressions. This chapter will show that regardless of the continued use of political microaggressions by political elites to disparage minorities, assimilation to "American" values continues to be strong. Second, an individual's country of origin is not necessarily problematic for most Americans.[10] However, to be considered "truly American," language skills are a factor—language, specifically English, seems to be more important than sharing national customs and traditions.[11] This last finding is significant because it underscores how various ethnic groups view the influence of other groups in American politics. The perception of minority group influence in American politics may be overstated as a result of nativist inclinations. Thus, political rhetoric that affirms false social stereotypes, biases, and prejudices against minority groups may lead to political microaggressions against minorities who seem to have a perceived disproportionate political advantage.

## Americanism—What Is It?

What is Americanism? What does it mean to be American? These two questions are difficult to answer because they involve a range of mores, values, and traditions from individuals in various economic, political, and social stratifications. Recall that the Founding Fathers unequivocally excluded certain groups from their meaning of who had the correct pedigree to be considered American. Consider elected officials such as Woodrow Wilson, an advocate of segregation and supporter of the Ku Klux Klan, who limited African Americans' ability to participate in the "American" dream. Franklin Delano Roosevelt, seen by many as a calming leader during the Great Depression and champion of New Deal Policies, was a figure whose national programs neglected African Americans and continued Mexican repatriation, and whose administration was aware of the extermination of Jews well before deciding to act. Or, consider Idaho governor Chase Clark who expressed his discontent with the idea of voluntary migration of Japanese Americans as a result of the Pearl Harbor attack and the designation of military areas primarily on the West Coast. Governor Clark was quoted as saying: "The Japs live like rats, breed like rats and act like rats. We don't want them buying or leasing land or becoming permanently located in our state."[12]

Some would argue that Americans have not evolved much since the comments of Wilson, Roosevelt, and Clark. Take for example the incidents in West Texas and Kansas City as a lack of progression. However, the 2016 American National Election Study (ANES) indicates that Americans may be making progress in accepting changing demographics and what it means to be an American. The findings indicate that if there is one area that seems to define Americanism, it is language. Of those surveyed, 51 percent indicated that to be truly American, it is important to speak English. Moreover, another 24 percent indicated that language is fairly important to be truly American. Overall, 75 percent of respondents felt that speaking English is essential for being truly American (Table 5.1). This is not to say that bilingualism or multilingualism is not accepted, just that the ability to speak English is important for being defined as American. Respondents were also asked whether "To be truly American it is important to follow America's customs and traditions" (Table 5.2). Only 62 percent of those surveyed thought following customs and traditions was "very to fairly important" to be truly American. This is significant, considering how various minority groups, especially new immigrants to the United States, are framed as unassimilable. The framing by political elites has been that changing demographics will create great divisions in American society because certain groups do not want to follow American customs and traditions. Microaggressions are used to frame these groups as existing on the fringes of society and suggest they should not be thought of as American. What is not apparent from the survey question in Table 5.2 is what customs and traditions respondents consider American. The 62 percent who indicated that following customs and traditions was "very to fairly important" to be truly American were not surveyed on what those specific customs and traditions are. It could be a combination of celebrating Christmas, enjoying the Fourth of July, eating barbecue, saying grace before a meal, or the ability to recite the Bill of Rights. Regardless, although Americans share many similarities, they are not monolithic in their interpretation of what it means to be an American.

Table 5.1   To Be Truly American It Is Important to Speak English

| Response label | Percentage |
| --- | --- |
| Very important | 51.21 |
| Fairly important | 24.21 |
| Not very important | 6.58 |
| Not important at all | 3.04 |
| Refused to answer | .37 |
| Don't know | .02 |
| Other | 14.56 |
| Total N | 4271 |

*Source*: American National Elections Studies, *The ANES Guide to Public Opinion and Electoral Behavior* (Ann Arbor: University of Michigan, Center for Political Studies and Stanford University, 2017).

Question wording: How important do you think the following is for being truly American: to be able to speak English.

Table 5.2   To Be Truly American It Is Important to Follow America's Customs and Traditions

| Response label | Percentage |
| --- | --- |
| Very important | 29.01 |
| Fairly important | 33.13 |
| Not very important | 16.97 |
| Not important at all | 5.69 |
| Refused to answer | .49 |
| Don't know | .14 |
| Other | 14.56 |
| Total N | 4271 |

*Source*: American National Elections Studies, *The ANES Guide to Public Opinion and Electoral Behavior* (Ann Arbor: University of Michigan, Center for Political Studies and Stanford University, 2017).

Question wording: To be truly American is it important to follow America's customs/traditions?

As we saw with Table 5.2, defining Americanism is a difficult task to undertake. Individuals may define Americanism as apple pie, the Constitution, and love of country, while others may prefer freedom of speech, the ability to speak English, and football. Defining what it means to be an American is multifaceted, with various possible responses. The political rhetoric in the 2016 U.S. presidential elections framed the idea of Americanism as Anglo Saxon. Microaggressions toward African Americans, Latinos, and Muslims were at full throttle during the 2016 election; thus, the expectation would be that being born in America is a key facet of being truly American. However, in the 2016 ANES, less than 50 percent of respondents indicated that it was 'very to fairly important' to have been born in the United States to be considered American (Table 5.3). Another 39 percent of respondents did not think it was very important to be born in the United States to be considered American. This finding seems to contradict the political rhetoric from the 2016 U.S. presidential election in which immigrants were framed as drug dealers, rapists, and terrorists. The "us versus them" framing was used to create divisiveness due to changing demographics, but these survey findings indicate that there is more acceptance and latitude in what it means to be truly American, and that not being born in America is not a significant issue for those individuals surveyed.

Table 5.4 illustrates that 51 percent of those surveyed by ANES do not consider having American ancestry to be an important factor to being truly American. The data indicates only 34 percent of respondents considered American ancestry "very to fairly important." This finding seems to contradict the thesis of Huntington's essay that immigrants erode Anglo-Protestant culture and American political values. From these findings nativism may be less pronounced than what is framed by political elites and the media. The case may be that Americans are more accepting of various cultures and place

**Table 5.3   To Be Truly American It Is Important to Have Been Born in the United States**

| Response label | Percentage |
| --- | --- |
| Very important | 21.33 |
| Fairly important | 24.02 |
| Not very important | 22.50 |
| Not important at all | 16.97 |
| Refused to answer | .49 |
| Don't know | .12 |
| Other | 14.56 |
| Total N | 4271 |

*Source*: American National Elections Studies, *The ANES Guide to Public Opinion and Electoral Behavior* (Ann Arbor: University of Michigan, Center for Political Studies and Stanford University, 2017).

Question wording: How important do you think the following is for being truly American: to have been born in the country.

**Table 5.4    To Be Truly American It Is Important to Have American Ancestry**

| Response label | Percentage |
|---|---|
| Very important | 12.46 |
| Fairly important | 21.70 |
| Not very important | 27.44 |
| Not important at all | 23.25 |
| Refused to answer | .44 |
| Don't know | .14 |
| Other | 14.56 |
| Total N | 4271 |

*Source*: American National Elections Studies, *The ANES Guide to Public Opinion and Electoral Behavior* (Ann Arbor: University of Michigan, Center for Political Studies and Stanford University, 2017).

Question wording: How important do you think the following is for being truly American: to have American ancestry.

less emphasis on ancestry when compared to other facets of Americanism, such as language.

The findings in Tables 5.1 through 5.4 show that to be thought of as truly American, various factors are considered. Of the responses presented, only the ability to speak English was an integral component of Americanism. This finding seems to indicate the growing number of minority groups may be more easily accepted if they have the ability to speak English. This in turn could be one of the factors that determine how growing minority groups are framed within the social context.

Table 5.5 highlights how various ethnic groups view the influence of other groups in American politics. Survey respondents were asked, "Which racial and ethnic groups influence American politics?" The responses were striking when we examine individual racial categories. Blacks, Hispanics, and Asians were seen as having "too little influence," while whites were seen as having "too much influence." Just as significant were the response rates for racial and ethnic groups with "just about the right amount of influence in American politics." Overwhelmingly, 50 percent of respondents indicated that whites had "just about the right amount of influence." However, when we take into account respondents who indicated "too much influence" and "just the right amount," the percentage increases to 78 percent of respondents indicating whites have "too much or just the right amount of influence" in American politics. This finding aligns with the number of non-Hispanic white elected officials at various levels of government. What does this mean

Table 5.5   Which Racial and Ethnic Groups Influence American Politics

| | Racial/ethnic groups | | | |
| --- | --- | --- | --- | --- |
| | Whites | Blacks | Hispanics | Asians |
| Too much influence | 28.71 | 7.82 | 5.88 | 2.60 |
| Just about the right amount of influence | 49.66 | 39.36 | 39.90 | 44.49 |
| Too little influence | 5.06 | 36.31 | 37.65 | 36.20 |
| Refused to answer | 1.29 | 1.22 | 1.29 | 1.43 |
| Other | 14.56 | 14.56 | 14.56 | 14.56 |
| Total N | 4271 | 4271 | 4271 | 4271 |

*Source*: American National Elections Studies, *The ANES Guide to Public Opinion and Electoral Behavior* (Ann Arbor: University of Michigan, Center for Political Studies and Stanford University, 2017).

Question wording: Would you say that [insert one of the following groups: whites, blacks, Hispanics, Asian Americans] have too much influence in American politics?

for growing minority groups or changing demographics? How will the interests of growing minority groups be represented by white elected officials? Do minority interests differ from those of whites? Or are we at a point in political history where changing demographics mean that minorities will demand a larger presence in politics?

## Is There Hope or Is It a Lost Cause?

The implications of political microaggressions targeted at minorities should not be discounted, especially in a changing racial environment. Future public policies and political debate are currently being framed as an "us versus them" problem in an effort to create divisiveness and infighting among and between groups of people. Divisiveness and infighting erodes trust in government, institutions, and people. Take for example, the birther movement touted by Donald Trump prior to his candidacy for president, in which he accused President Obama of providing a fraudulent birth certificate,[13] of not being born in the United States, and of being Muslim. In an interview with Sean Hannity of Fox News, Trump made the following claims:

> **Sean Hannity, Host**: Tonight is part two of my interview with potential 2012 presidential candidate Donald Trump who has been making headlines for the controversial rebukes that he has issued President Obama. And that's where we begin tonight. Let's take a look.

(Begin video clip)

**Hannity**: A lot has been made over the birth certificate issue. And you apparently, you have said in previous interviews that you have a team of investigators in Hawaii now looking into it.

**Donald Trump, Businessman**: Correct.

**Hannity**: It has a lot of press. Everyone is asking you about it.

**Trump**: Right.

**Hannity**: And what have you come up with in your investigations?

**Trump**: Well, I don't want to say that now. But it is going to be very interesting. But I don't want to say it now, Sean. But I will say this, I don't love this issue. I'd much rather be talking about how China is ripping us off, how OPEC is—that's what I'm really good at. I understand it. I can do such a great job.

But, this issue came up about six weeks ago. And I've heard about it for years. But I never thought too much about it. And I assumed he was born in this country. But six weeks ago, I started really looking into it. He's got a certificate of live birth. That's, by the way, despite what certain liberal press says, that's not a birth certificate. It is a big, big step lower. In fact, in some places, you can get married or get a driver's license with a certificate of live birth, OK? So, I say to myself, why?

**Hannity:** Only has a stamp, no signature.

**Trump:** It's got a stamp. It's got a stamp. No, it's got a stamped signature. By the way, I have my birth certificate. I think I'll show it. I think I'm going to bring it down to Boca Raton this weekend. But I have my, it's got stamps, it's got three different signatures, it's got everything, everything is official. You have to see this thing. It's like a certificate of live birth is not appropriate.[14]

If the first African American elected to the U.S. presidency can be the recipient of racist microaggressions and falsely accused of not being an American, what hope is there for other minorities? Moreover, if as I have argued above, a growing number of minorities are being framed as an "us versus them" in a microaggressive environment, is there hope that economic, social, and political equality will prevail?

Eduardo Bonilla-Silva uses the term *racial optimists* to describe "groups of analysts who agree with whites' common sense on racial matters and believe the changes symbolize a profound transition in the United States."[15] Bonilla-Silva argues that since the late 1950s surveys on racial attitudes continue to indicate that fewer whites subscribe to attitudes that align with Jim Crow and that fewer whites have stereotypic views about African Americans.[16] Similarly, Howard Schuman, Charlotte Steeh, and Lawrence Bobo found similar results in their analysis of how well Americans accept racial equality and to what extent racism still exists. The team of scholars found that in the 1940s it was common for whites to support segregation at various levels of society (e.g., education, housing, employment), but by the 1980s less than a quarter of white respondents held the same view.[17] For example, survey respondents from 1942 through 1983 were asked about integrating schools: "Do you think white students and black students should go to the same school or separate schools?" In the 1940s and 1950s the majority supported separate schools, but by 1982, nine out of 10 Americans supported school integration.[18] This same trend was found for questions involving public accommodations, employment opportunities, and seating on public transportation. These findings seem to indicate that there was a semblance of hope and less antipathy toward racial minorities, specifically blacks, when compared to the Jim Crow era and the 1940s and 1950s.

Thirty years later we seem to be asking the same question, but in a different context. In 2016, the Pew Research Center released its report on racial views between blacks and whites. The results show a divide in perceptions of how different races are treated. Over 60 percent of blacks surveyed indicated that they were treated less fairly in their interactions with police, the court system, when applying for loans, and in the workplace,[19] while only 50 and 43 percent of whites thought blacks were treated less fairly in their interactions with police and the court system.[20] Furthermore, the results indicate that blacks and whites have different perspectives on race relations in the United States. Over 60 percent of blacks indicated that race relations were bad, while only 45 percent of whites indicated race relations were bad.[21] More significant, in 2008, the United States elected its first African American president, Barack Obama. There was a euphoric sense of accomplishment that after so many years of racial strife, maybe the United States was evolving in its race relations. However, the 2016 Pew survey indicates otherwise. Thirty-two percent of whites indicated that the election of the first African American president made race relations worse—62 percent of whom were white Republicans.[22] The survey further revealed a sizeable divide in regard to race relations among whites based on political party affiliation. Fifty-nine percent of white Republicans indicated too much attention was paid to race and racial issues, whereas 49 percent of white Democrats thought too little attention was being paid to race.[23]

When we look back at the early surveys and compare them to the 2016 survey, what does this mean for our current state of affairs and the use of hostile political rhetoric entwined with microaggressions to divide people? Is there hope or is it a lost cause? As Paul B. Sheatsley, a prominent authority on public opinion polling, concluded:

> The mass of white Americans have shown in many ways that they will not follow a racist government and that they will not follow racist leaders.

Rather, they are engaged in the painful task of adjusting to an integrated society. It will not be easy for most, but one cannot at this late date doubt the basic commitment. In their hearts they know that the American Negro is right.[24]

While Paul B. Sheatsley's comments were directed toward race relations between whites and African Americans, this same principle can be applied to our current unconventional state of politics. The majority of Americans will not follow a racist government or leader. Most Americans will want to push back against microaggressions and the use of political rhetoric as a weapon; thus hope is the preferred alternative.

## Conclusion

Will political microaggressions continue to be used to create a framework of "us versus them" in order to obfuscate minority interests? Not only are minority interests at risk of not being represented, but so are the interests of all Americans regardless of race or ethnicity. In a 1978 speech to College Republicans, then candidate for Congress Newt Gingrich made the following remarks:

> And I think that one of the great problems we have in the Republican Party is that we don't encourage you to be nasty. We encourage you to be neat, obedient, and loyal and faithful and all those Boy Scout words, which would be great around the campfire, but are lousy in politics. . . .
>
> One of the great weaknesses of the Republican party is we recruit middle-class people. Middle-class people, as a group, are told you should not shout at the table, you should be nice, you should have respect for other people, which usually means giving way to them. . . .
>
> All of you should know that by now you're old enough to know that all human beings are weak and frail and occasionally tempted, probably even one or two of you have been tempted. So you don't want to trust politicians, you want to hold them accountable. You want to be able to say to them, "We have a contractual relationship, based on that I am a stockholder for you in your campaign, and if you do not listen to me and do something," I don't mean that they're going to obey you like a puppet, but at least understand where your problems are, "If you're not going to listen to me and honor me, then I'm going to sell my stock in you and I'm going to invest in somebody else and we're going to beat you."[25]

Gingrich's speech in 1978 raises several questions that are still pertinent in 2018. First, do we want to continue to elect politicians that are "nasty?" As I have established, politics is not for the faint of heart, but should citizens continue to elect officials who perpetuate the cyclical nature of microaggressions against groups when history shows that only one group benefits—the 1 percent of Americans who hold all the wealth in the United States? Second, we must consider the recruitment of the middle-class into politics. Gingrich argues "one of the great weaknesses of the Republican party is we recruit middle-class people." Gingrich insinuates that the middle class is too nice and is willing to compromise when they should not. Why is it acceptable for our elected officials not to want to compromise with their colleagues? In any other profession, the inability to work well with others will be noted on annual reviews and may lead to termination of employment. So why is the inability to compromise an acceptable position for elected officials who represent various constituents who may share similarities but are not monolithic? Third, Gingrich argues that "you don't want to trust politicians, you want to hold them accountable." We should all heed this advice. Hold politicians accountable and resist the temptation to trust them, especially when they engage in the use of microaggressions to accentuate differences between groups and when they use political rhetoric to negatively frame certain groups. Point three will be important to consider as demographics continue to change to a plurality minority population.

# CHAPTER SIX

# Trump: Unconventionality in the White House

@GovernorPerry failed on the border. He should be forced to take an IQ test before being allowed to enter the GOP debate.[1]

I just realized that if you listen to Carly Fiorina for more than ten minutes straight, you develop a massive headache. She has zero chance![2]

@SenJohnMcCain should be defeated in the primaries. Graduated last in his class at Annapolis—dummy![3]

It wasn't the White House, it wasn't the State Department, it wasn't father LaVar's so-called people on the ground in China that got his son out of a long term prison sentence—IT WAS ME. Too bad! LaVar is just a poor man's version of Don King, but without the hair. Just think.[4]

How unconventional is Trump, and what is the Trump effect? And what has happened in society that we are experiencing the unconventional Trump effect? Consider how unconventional Trump was as a candidate and is as a president. Some people experience elation when Trump engages in a micro-aggression via a tweet or verbal comment; others have a pit-in-their-stomach feeling when they watch the news or grab their mobile devices, anticipating that Trump has lashed out at someone or engaged in questionable behavior. At this point in our political history, the most unconventional elected leader of modern time is the president of the United States. Prior to the 2016 U.S. presidential election, Trump made no qualms about his political stance, his political rhetoric, or his temperament. So why do some individuals feel that they have been "sucker punched in the gut" with Trump as an elected leader? Because Trump is unfiltered, brash, and unapologetic, but more importantly because he won the election with questionable attributes. Trump is by no means the only political figure perpetrating microaggressions, but he is certainly the most visible person at the moment. In this chapter, I will explore why some voters suggest that Trump is "getting away with it" and why now is the time in American history that we feel comfortable electing a president who at times behaves unpresidentially. I will also explore the idea of confronting microaggression in an unconventional political era. The use of political microaggressions in politics is important to consider because negative political rhetoric is successful at creating spaces where ordinary American citizens and elected officials feel indifferent about posting hostile rhetoric on social media or espousing denigrating views about others in interviews, which can lead to divisiveness and continued inequitable socioeconomic public policies.

## Why Is Trump "Getting Away with It"?

Elected officials, the media, and scholars in multiple academic fields have all attempted to rationalize the election of Donald J. Trump. Part of the rationalization process is figuring out why Trump continues to "get away" with blatant microaggressions and questionable behavior. The most commonly accepted theory is that citizens have become disillusioned with government.[5] According to Arlie Russell Hochschild, a sociologist at the University of California, Berkeley, who befriended and interviewed Tea Party members in Louisiana over a five-year period, as a country the United States has been moving apart, and the percentage of individuals who identify with the message from right-wing politics has continued to grow.[6] Throughout her five years in Louisiana, Hochschild began to understand the phenomenon of emotion in politics—how right-wing politics tap into the feelings and mindset of some individuals. At the same time Hochschild was conducting her research, Trump was nominated as the Republican candidate for the U.S. presidency, allowing Hochschild to capture the emotions of right-wing voters at its core. One main question that Hochschild asked participants was "Why do you hate government, you know all the things government does?" In general, the response was almost always the same: respondents were tired of being left behind and tired of other groups forcing their views on them. Hochschild also acknowledges that "race was an essential part of this story,"[7] meaning that other races and ethnicities were prospering economically, socially, and politically at higher rates than most whites in Louisiana. Hochschild describes the support for Trump by Louisianans in the following way:

> The deep story of the right, the *feels-as-if* story, corresponds to a real structural squeeze. People want to achieve the American dream, but for a mixture

of reasons feel they are being held back, and this leads people of the right to feel frustrated, angry, and betrayed by the government. Race is an essential part of this story.[8]

All this was part of the "deep story." In that story, strangers step ahead of you in line, making you anxious, resentful, and afraid. A president [in reference to President Obama] allies with the line cutters, making you feel distrustful, betrayed. A person ahead of you in line insults you as an ignorant redneck, making you feel humiliated and mad. Economically, culturally, demographically, politically, you are suddenly a stranger in your own land. The whole context of Louisiana—its companies, its government, its church and media—reinforces that deep story. So this—the deep story—was in place before the media was struck.[9]

Trump is an "emotions candidate." More than any other presidential candidate in decades, Trump focuses on eliciting and praising emotional responses from his fans rather than detailed policy prescriptions. His speeches—evoking dominance, bravado, clarity, national pride, and personal uplift—inspire an emotional transformation. Then he *points* to that transformation. "We have passion," he told the Louisiana gathering. "We're not silent anymore; we're the loud, noisy majority." He derides his rivals in both parties for their inability to inspire enthusiasm. "They lack energy." Not only does Trump evoke emotion, he makes an object of it, presenting it back to his fans as a sign of collective success.

His supporters have been in mourning for a lost way of life. Many have become discouraged, others depressed. They yearn to feel pride but instead have felt shame. Their land no longer feels their own. Joined together with others like themselves, they now feel hopeful, joyous, elated. The man who expressed amazement, arms upheld—"to be in the presence of such a man!"—seemed in a state of rapture. As if magically lifted, *they are no longer strangers in their own land*.[10]

Hochschild's analysis could serve as an explanation for why Trump is able to get away with the use of microaggressions. Trump's microaggressions are what some people feel and think at a core level. What should not be overlooked in Hochschild's work is her comment that "race was an essential part of the story." Hochschild goes on to state that most of the individuals she interviewed did not think of themselves as racists. "They thought of racism as instances where you hate blacks or where you use the N-word. And they didn't hate blacks, and they didn't use the N-word, and so they didn't feel like racists. They didn't look at, you know, could you get an apartment in Trump Towers or, you know, government benefits after World War II, that kind of thing."[11]

Recall from Chapter 2 that growing minority populations have the potential of changing government institutions, laws, and the political process. As a result, Tea Party Louisianans are attuned to the changing ethnic balance and political environment precipitated by the growth in African American, Asian American, Latino, and immigrant populations. For some Tea Party Louisianans, the constant reminder of changing demographics exacerbates the need to keep the United States monolithic. The natural inclination becomes protecting communities against growing minority groups that threaten the American way of life. Thus, Trump and his use of nativist rhetoric is what appeals to them—consequently, Trump can get away with blatant microaggressions and questionable behavior if it creates conditions where the economic, social, and political order puts his supporters at the front of the line, instead of the back of the line—a place historically reserved for minority populations.

### Why Is Now the Time in American History That We Feel Comfortable Electing a President Who Behaves Like This?

There has been abundant commentary and theories on why some citizens feel comfortable with Donald J. Trump as president. In focus groups, at conferences, at dinner tables, at sporting events, in churches, and in many other places there have been discussions about how and why Trump was elected. Possible explanations include: white middle class Americas feel that they have been ignored by government; too many immigrants are changing the fabric of what it means to be an American living in America; Americans have become too politically correct; the need to make America a great defensive powerhouse again; the theory that government only advocates for minorities and not other hardworking groups; the idea that Trump will make America great again; Trump was the lesser of two evils; all politicians are crooked and Trump as an outsider can't be any worse; he's a rich businessman and will bring jobs back; and finally, Trump's anti-immigrant, anti-Muslim, pro-Confederate language continues to appeal to some voters. For citizens who have concerns about one or more of these issues, Trump is seen as the panacea that can remedy their concerns. Supporters will overlook Trump's use of microaggressions as long as he continues to verbally reiterate microaggressions that resonate with them.

From an academic perspective, there has been an enormous increase in research on Trump, the Trump effect, and the circumstances that led to Trump being elected. Robert Reich, professor of public policy at the University of Berkeley and former secretary of labor in the Clinton administration, argues, "in coming years the major fault in American politics will shift from Democrat versus Republican to an anti-establishment versus establishment—that is, to the middle class, working class, and the poor who see the game as rigged versus the executives of large corporations, the inhabitants of Wall Street, and the billionaires who do the rigging."[12] Reich maintains that the feeling of dissatisfaction with government some Americans experience is due in large part to economics and the idea that corporate America is getting richer and everyone else is getting left behind. Reich's argument seems to align with one of the campaign slogans Trump used to appeal to middle-class Americans, "It's time to drain the swamp." Trump was referring to imposing more restrictions on revolving-door politics by lobbyists in order to minimize the influence lobbying groups have on elected officials. Essentially, Trump's idea was getting rid of a corrupt system that influenced policies that only benefited 1 percent of the U.S. population. Asymmetrical economic conditions seem to have created a receptive audience to Trump's economic promises, setting up a social and political environment where microaggressions and indiscretions are overlooked in hopes of achieving economic parity.

Other scholars have argued that Trump was elected because the Latino vote that for years has been seen as changing politics in America was not a viable factor in the 2016 presidential election. Rodolfo de la Garza, a professor of political science at Columbia University, stated:

And if I'm right, and I'll bet money that I'm right, Latinos will be absolutely irrelevant in this election. So there aren't many states where there's enough Latinos, where the margin's going to be so tight that Latinos make a difference. Hillary's going to win California, and Hillary, I don't think, will win Texas—both huge Latino states. And there will be a lot of people voting against Trump, not necessarily for Hillary. And Latinos will be in that group, but that group will be bigger than Latinos.[13]

Scholars such as political science researchers Michael Barber and Jeremy Pope at Brigham Young University challenged the conventional academic notion that citizens hold consistent ideological political views.[14] In nonacademic terms, Barber and Pope challenged the established norm that policy preferences of citizens in regard to liberal and conservative issues remain consistent over time and are based on principles and values that are not easily changed. Barber and Pope used YouGov 2017 survey data that was collected immediately after the inauguration of Donald Trump, where survey participants were asked a number of questions regarding their political positions on various issues. Their findings revealed that when Trump provided cues on a range of issues, Republicans moved their ideological political views in the same direction as Trump's cue. If Trump provided a liberal or conservative cue on an issue, Republicans shifted their view to align with Trump, which suggests that party loyalty rather than ideological cues may be stronger than previously established.[15] For some Trump supporters, policy preferences are secondary to party preferences, since they easily shift their ideological views on an array of political issues to match those of the party leader. These preliminary findings may be one of many explanations for why some voters feel comfortable electing a president known for his relentless use of verbal microaggressions. It is not necessarily about the issues, but about what the party stands for (in this case the Republican Party) and how comfortable some people are in shifting their ideological preferences to the candidate and party they support.

## Imperceptive Panacea Influence

Another rationale for why some citizens feel comfortable electing a president who engages in microaggressions and hostile political rhetoric is that Trump is seen as the panacea or "cure all" who can "fix" the political distress and distrust in government and "Make America Great Again."[16] I refer to this as the *imperceptive panacea influence* (IPI) or the "cure-all influence." IPI can take one of two forms: the unintentional lack of awareness or discernment about certain actions, and the intentional awareness and discernment about certain actions. In the first form of IPI, an individual may not have the political awareness or capacity to disentangle policy issues and/or the ability to decipher political rhetoric that a candidate or elected official has engaged in; thus they unintentionally acquiesce to an individual as being a panacea or a "cure" for the problem. The second form of IPI is more deliberate; an individual is aware of or has some understanding of politics and or policy issues. Consciously and on a larger scale, individuals in this second form have some understanding of politics and the role of government—this is coupled with the capacity to identify overt deleterious political rhetoric and hostile behavior. This form of IPI is more calculated and dangerous since individuals in this group intentionally self-select to ignore and/or minimize microaggressive actions of candidates or elected officials. For an individual in this second form of IPI, toxic political rhetoric and negative behavior is what attracts them to a candidate. An individual internally makes the conscious decision to support an individual who espouses negative rhetoric and behavior that resonates with their personal viewpoints, but outwardly these individuals try to hide or conceal their true feelings from others. When a candidate or elected official engages in hostile political rhetoric and/or behavior, individuals in this group are motivated to support them regardless of their political or party identification.

Because Trump has been successful in framing the types of public policies that are important to some voters, he has been able to change the tone of public policy issues while at the same time offering some type of policy remedy (i.e., IPI). From illegal immigration to building "the Wall" between the United States and Mexico to the travel ban that barred international citizens from eight countries from traveling to the United States—Trump is seen as the "cure all" for these "ailments." Additionally, Trump has galvanized and accelerated nationalist sentiments with his "Make America Great Again"

Table 6.1   Americans' Favorable Ratings of Putin, by Party

|              | 2015 | 2017 | Change   |
|--------------|------|------|----------|
|              | %    | %    | pct. pts. |
| Republicans  | 12   | 32   | +20      |
| Independents | 12   | 23   | +11      |
| Democrats    | 15   | 10   | −5       |

*Source*: Art Swift, "Putin's Image Rises in U.S., Mostly Among Republicans," Gallup, February 21, 2017, http://news.gallup.com /poll/204191/putin-image-rises-mostly-among-republicans.aspx.

rhetoric. This has resulted in some citizens approving of his use of Twitter to post microaggressions and engage in hostile political rhetoric—the second form of IPI. For instance, many polls continue to show that Trump's political base remains supportive regardless of his use of microaggressions on Twitter, his verbal attacks against members of his own party, and attacks against those outside of the Republican Party. For this set of voters, Trump is considered the solution to the problem, and because of this, he can frame how public policy issues are perceived.

Recall that individuals in the second form of IPI are aware of or have some understanding of politics and/or policy issues and consciously self-select to ignore and/or minimize certain behaviors. So when a political issue is framed as unimportant, which can include issues such as understating Russian government interference in the 2016 presidential election, individuals in this second form of IPI go along with how Trump frames the issue. As a result, numerous polls continue to indicate that there is consistent support for Trump regardless of his microaggressions or Russian interference in the election.[17] For example, polling data shows that in 2017 Americans had a more favorable view of Russian president Vladimir Putin when compared to 2015. Table 6.1 indicates that in 2015 only 12 percent of Republicans and Independents had a favorable view of President Putin, but by 2017 a favorable view of Putin increased to 32 and 23 percent.

The favorable rate of approval for Putin is significant because multiple substantiated investigations have confirmed that the Russian government was successful in interfering in the 2016 presidential election, which favored the Republican candidate.[18] In November 2017, the U.S. intelligence community, which included CIA Director Mike Pompeo, appointed by Donald Trump, acknowledged Russia interfered in the 2016 presidential election.[19] In addition, the U.S. Senate Intelligence Committee, one of several committees charged with investigating Russian interference in the election, released a report in September 2017 supporting the findings of the intelligence community that Russia sought to influence the 2016 U.S. presidential campaign.[20]

Trump for his part has expressed skepticism and has downplayed Russian interference in the election. Trump has pushed back against substantiated claims of Russian interference in the election and has diverted attention about the investigations by framing other issues as more important, while maintaining the support of his base (second form of IPI) as shown in Table 6.1. Here are a few of President Trump's tweets on these issues:

> Interesting to watch Senator Richard Blumenthal of Connecticut talking about hoax Russian collusion when he was a phony Vietnam con artist![21]

> @foxandfriends According to report just out, President Obama knew about Russian interference 3 years ago but he didn't want to anger Russia![22]

> The Russia hoax continues, now it's ads on Facebook. What about the totally biased and dishonest Media coverage in favor of Crooked Hillary.[23]

> All of this "Russia" talk about when the Republicans are making their big push for historic tax Cuts & Reform. Is this coincidental? NOT![24]

> . . .the Uranium to Russia deal, the 33,000 plus deleted Emails, the Comey fix and so much more. Instead they look at phony Trump/Russia. . .[25]

> He said he didn't meddle [in regard to Vladimir Putin], I asked him again. You can only ask so many times. I just asked him again. He said he absolutely did not meddle in our election. He did not do what they are saying he did. Every time he sees me he says, 'I didn't do that,' and I really believe that when he tells me that, he means it. I think he is very insulted by it, which is not a good thing for our country.[26]

Table 6.2 shows Americans' favorable rating of Putin by party identification and by education. This table indicates that support for Putin is strong when education is not considered, but when education is considered, support for Putin diminishes. For instance, individuals with a high school education or less experienced the largest change in support for Putin between February 2017 to June 2017. This group's support fell from 28 to 16 percent, a change of negative 12 percentage points. The case may be that this group of individuals aligns more closely with the first form of IPI where an individual may not have the political awareness or capacity to disentangle policy issues and unintentionally acquiesces to an individual as being a panacea for the problem. However, because this group does not self-select to ignore and/or minimize microaggressive actions by candidates or elected officials, eventually these people may begin to distance themselves from an elected official, resulting in less support for Putin. For individuals in this first form of IPI, the original framing of Russian interference may have run its course, resulting in a less favorable view of the Russian president. Overall, the largest percentage

Table 6.2    Americans' Favorable Ratings of Putin, by Party and Education

|  | Feb 2017 | June 2017 | Change |
|---|---|---|---|
|  | % | % | pct. pts. |
| **Party ID** | | | |
| Republicans | 32 | 24 | −8 |
| Independents | 23 | 12 | −11 |
| Democrats | 10 | 4 | −6 |
| **Education** | | | |
| Postgraduate | 13 | 6 | −7 |
| College graduate | 13 | 7 | −6 |
| Some college | 23 | 16 | −7 |
| High school or less | 28 | 16 | −12 |

*Source*: Art Swift, "Putin's Already Negative U.S. Image Worsens," Gallup, June 23, 2017, http://news.gallup.com/poll/212744/putin-already-negative-image-worsens.aspx.

point changes occurred with individuals with a high school education or less. Interestingly, individuals with a college degree and postgraduate degree continue to view Putin favorably regardless of substantiated reports of the Russian interference. This group may align more closely with the second form of IPI, where they self-select to continue to view Putin favorably.

From this we can infer two things: one, Trump has been successful in framing Russian interference in the election as a nonfactor in his election, for individuals in both the first and second form of IPI. This is demonstrated in Tables 6.1 by the rate of approval by Republicans and Independents for President Putin regardless of Russian interference in the 2016 presidential election. The rate of approval for Putin is 20 and 11 percentage points higher in Feb. 2017 when compared to the 2015 Americans' favorable ratings of Putin, by party poll. The second thing we can infer is that the second form of IPI is indeed very strong for some individuals. Recall, the second form of IPI is conscious, deliberate, and dangerous, and individuals self-select to ignore and/or minimize the microaggressive actions of candidates or elected officials (e.g., Tea Party Louisianans). Individuals are more calculating in their support for individuals with whom they inwardly connect, while outwardly these individuals try to conceal their true outlooks from others (e.g., Tea Party Louisianans). Since the election of Donald Trump, many polls continue to indicate that staunch supporters are not ready to abandon the president. The case may be that Trump's microaggressive behavior is what attracts individuals in the second form of IPI. The second form of IPI may be a latent factor that has created social and political conditions conducive to why some citizens feel comfortable with Donald J. Trump as president.

## Confronting Microaggressions in an Unconventional Political Era

Although Trump has experienced continued support from members of his own party at various levels of government, there have been several occasions where members of his own party have opposed Trump's microaggression tactics. Some elected officials have pushed back harder than others, and it is unusual, to say the least, to find members of the president's own political party openly expressing their discontent with the president. Moreover, before the election of Trump, several members of the Republican Party openly opposed Trump as presidential candidate. Senator Ben Sasse (R-NE) posted the following message to Trump supporters on his Facebook page:

AN OPEN LETTER TO TRUMP SUPPORTERS

To my friends supporting Donald Trump:

The Trump coalition is broad and complicated, but I believe many Trump fans are well-meaning. I have spoken at length with many of you, both inside and outside Nebraska. You are rightly worried about our national direction. You ache about a crony-capitalist leadership class that is not urgent about tackling our crises. You are right to be angry.

I'm as frustrated and saddened as you are about what's happening to our country. But I cannot support Donald Trump.

Please understand: I'm not an establishment Republican, and I will never support Hillary Clinton. I'm a movement conservative who was elected over the objections of the GOP establishment. My current answer for who I would support in a hypothetical matchup between Mr. Trump and Mrs. Clinton is: Neither of them. I sincerely hope we select one of the other GOP candidates, but if Donald Trump ends up as the GOP nominee, conservatives will need to find a third option.

Mr. Trump's relentless focus is on dividing Americans, and on tearing down rather than building back up this glorious nation. Much like President Obama, he displays essentially no understanding of the fact that, in the American system, we have a constitutional system of checks and balances, with three separate but co-equal branches of government. And the task of public officials is to be public "servants." The law is king, and the people are boss. But have you noticed how Mr. Trump uses the word "Reign"—like he thinks he's running for King? It's creepy, actually. Nebraskans are not looking for a king. We yearn instead for the recovery of a Constitutional Republic.[27]

In addition, Trump's use of microaggressions while in the White House has spurred some members of the Senate to speak out against his tactics. Take for example, the comments made during a live interview with CNN cable news by Senator Bob Corker (R-TN), a member of the Foreign Relations Committee:

**Manu Raju (CNN):** Do you regret supporting him [Donald Trump] in the election?

**Senator Corker:** Uh, let's just put it this way, I would not do it again.

**Manu Raju (CNN):** You wouldn't support him again?

**Senator Corker:** No way. No way. I think that he's proven himself unable to rise to the occasion, I think many of us, me included, have tried to . . . I've intervened, I've had a private dinner, I've been with him on multiple occasions to try to create some kind of aspirational . . . approach if you will, to the way that he conducts himself. But I don't think that that's possible and he's obviously not going to rise to the occasion as president.

**Manu Raju (CNN):** Do you think he's a role model to children in the United States?

**Senator Corker:** No.

**Manu Raju (CNN):** You don't.

**Senator Corker:** No. Absolutely not. I think that the things that are happening right now that are harmful to our nation, whether it's the breaking down of . . . we're gonna be doing some hearings on some of the things that he purposely is breaking down the relationships we have around the world that have been useful to our nation.

But I think at the end of the day when his term is over, I think the debasing of our nation, the constant non-truth-telling, just the name calling, I think the debasement of our nation will be what he'll be remembered most for, and that's regretful.

And it affects young people. I mean, we have young people who for the first time are watching a president stating absolute non-truths nonstop. Personalizing things in the way that he does. And it's very sad for our nation.[28]

Other senators have also taken issue with Trump's rhetoric, including John McCain and Jeff Flake. John McCain, Arizona's Republican senator, wrote an op-ed in the *Washington Post* in which he rebukes President Trump's speech and conduct. Following is an excerpt of McCain's op-ed:

Our entire system of government—with its checks and balances, its bicameral Congress, its protections of the rights of the minority—was designed for compromise. It seldom works smoothly or speedily. It was never expected to.

It requires pragmatic problem-solving from even the most passionate partisans. It relies on compromise between opposing sides to protect the interests we share. We can fight like hell for our ideas to prevail. But we have to respect each other or at least respect the fact that we need each other.

That has never been truer than today, when Congress must govern with a president who has no experience of public office, is often poorly informed and can be impulsive in his speech and conduct. We must respect his authority and constitutional responsibilities. We must, where we can, cooperate with him. But we are not his subordinates. We don't answer to him. We answer to the American people.[29]

In another instance, on October 24, 2017, Jeff Flake, the Republican senator from Arizona, announced on the Senate floor that he would not seek reelection in 2018. Flake, a conservative member of the Senate, took the opportunity to deliver a 17-minute speech condemning Donald Trump and his hostile style of politics. In his retirement speech, Flake spoke about the reckless and dangerous behavior emanating from the executive branch and urged his colleagues not to remain silent, saying, "We know better than that." Following is an excerpt from Senator Flake's speech, confronting the numerous incidents of microaggressions espoused by the president of the United States:

At a moment when it seems that our democracy is more defined by our discord and our dysfunction than by our own values and principles, let me begin by noting the somewhat obvious point that these offices that we hold are not ours indefinitely. We are not here simply to mark time. Sustained incumbency is certainly not the point of seeking office and there are times when we must risk our careers in favor of our principles. Now is such a time.

It must also be said that I rise today with no small measure of regret. Regret because of the state of our disunion. Regret because of the disrepair and destructiveness of our politics. Regret because of the indecency of our discourse. Regret because of the coarseness of our leadership.

Regret for the compromise of our moral authority, and by our, I mean all of our complicity in this alarming and dangerous state of affairs. It is time for our complicity and our accommodation of the unacceptable to end. In this century, a new phrase has entered the language to describe the accommodation of a new and undesirable order, that phrase being the new normal.

But we must never adjust to the present coarseness of our national dialogue with the tone set up at the top. We must never regard as normal the regular and casual undermining of our democratic norms and ideals. We must never meekly accept the daily sundering of our country. The personal attacks, the threats against principles, freedoms and institution, the flagrant disregard for truth and decency.

The reckless provocations, most often for the pettiest and most personal reasons, reasons having nothing whatsoever to do with the fortunes of the people that we have been elected to serve. None of these appalling features of our current politics should ever be regarded as normal. We must never allow ourselves to lapse into thinking that that is just the way things are now.

If we simply become inured to this condition, thinking that it is just politics as usual, then heaven help us. Without fear of the consequences and without consideration of the rules of what is politically safe or palatable, we must stop pretending that the degradation of our politics and the conduct of some in our executive branch are normal. They are not normal. Reckless, outrageous and undignified behavior has become excused and countenanced as telling it like it is when it is actually just reckless, outrageous and undignified.

And when such behavior emanates from the top of our government, it is something else. It is dangerous to a democracy. Such behavior does not project strength because our strength comes from our values. It instead projects a corruption of the spirit and weakness. It is often said that children are watching. Well, they are. And what are we going to do about that? When the next generation asks us, "Why didn't you do something? Why didn't you speak up?" What are we going to say?

Mr. President, I rise today to say: enough.[30]

Similarly, on October 19, 2017, former U.S. president George W. Bush, in his speech at The Spirit of Liberty: At Home, In The World, a national forum on freedom and security held in New York City, denounced the act of bullying and bigotry from the highest levels of leadership in the United States.[31] In his speech, Bush did not name current president Donald J. Trump outright, but the inference was clear that U.S. leadership plays a role in setting the political tone, not only in politics, but also in upholding democratic values. Bush addressed the issue of Russian interference in the 2016 presidential elections and the responsibility to pass on civic values to others, and called on institutions at all levels to provide cultural and moral leadership:

In recent decades, public confidence in our institutions has declined. . . . The American dream of upward mobility seems out of reach for some who have been left behind in a changing economy. Discontent deepened and sharpened partisan conflicts. Bigotry seems emboldened. Our politics seems more vulnerable to conspiracy theories and outright fabrication.

There are some signs that the intensity of support for democracy itself has waned, especially among the young . . .

Our country must show resolve and resilience in the face of external attacks on our democracy. And that begins with confronting a new era of cyber threats.

America is experiencing a sustained attempt by a hostile power to feed and exploit our country's divisions. According to our intelligence services, the Russian government has made a project of turning Americans against each other. This effort is broad, systematic and stealthy, it's conducted across a range of social media platforms. Ultimately, this assault won't succeed. But foreign aggressions—including cyber attacks, disinformation, and financial influence—should not be downplayed or tolerated. This is a clear case where the strength of our democracy begins at home. We must secure our electoral infrastructure and protect our electoral system from subversion. . . .

Our identity as a nation—unlike many other nations—is not determined by geography or ethnicity, by soil or blood. Being an American involves the embrace of high ideals and civic responsibility. We become the heirs of Thomas Jefferson by accepting the ideal of human dignity found in the Declaration of Independence. We become the heirs of James Madison by understanding the genius and values of the U.S. Constitution. We become the heirs of Martin Luther King Jr. by recognizing one another not by the color of their skin, but by the content of their character.

This means that people of every race, religion, and ethnicity can be fully and equally American. It means that bigotry or white supremacy in any form is blasphemy against the American creed. . . .

Bullying and prejudice in our public life sets a national tone, provides permission for cruelty and bigotry, and compromises the moral education of children. The only way to pass along civic values is to first live up to them.

Finally, the Call to Action calls on major institutions of our democracy, public and private, to consciously and urgently attend to the problem of declining trust.

For example, our democracy needs a media that is transparent, accurate, and fair. Our democracy needs religious institutions that demonstrate integrity and champion civil discourse. Our democracy needs institutions of higher learning that are examples of truth and free expression.

In short, it is time for American institutions to step up and provide cultural and moral leadership for this nation.[32]

The speech by former President George W. Bush and the comments delivered by Senators Sasse, Corker, McCain, and Flake show that some members of the Republican Party at various levels of government are attempting to confront microaggressions in an unconventional political era. While these are not the only elected officials who have spoken out against Trump's microaggressions, it remains to be seen if other Republican leaders will follow their lead. The reality of this unconventional political era is that some elected officials, those in the second form of IPI, will continue to support Trump because his microaggressive rhetoric resonates with what they feel and think. As Hochschild pointed out, "race is an essential part of this story," and part of that stems from the continued demographic changes occurring across the United States. Microaggressions and questionable behavior will be tolerated if they result in an economic, social, and political order where certain groups are moved to the front of the line, as opposed to their perspective that they are at the back of the line.

## Conclusion

There are several factors that have created conditions where now is the time in American history when some voters feel comfortable electing a president whose behavior is questionable. Demographics have begun to change in the United States, resulting in shifting public policies—subsequently leading to economic, social, and political changes. The continued growth in economic stratification negatively magnifies changes in economic and social order. While 1 percent of the population continues to hold an enormous economic advantage over other groups (i.e., the rich are getting richer), the poor and middle class are competing with one another. When the perception exists and is amplified by an elected leader that someone in a "lesser group" is receiving more assistance from the government, the fear of "being left behind" becomes real. Thus, Trump's anti-immigrant and nativist comments appeal to some voters who feel that they have been left behind by a broken government system and that their voice has become muted in the process.

Coupling this with individuals who can be categorized as being in the first or second form of IPI makes this unconventional political era suitable for some individuals who feel comfortable electing a president who engages in microaggressive behavior. Individuals in the second form of IPI are disingenuous about changing demographics and hostile political rhetoric—they like what they hear. While some individuals may feel downtrodden and exasperated at the idea of a U.S. president behaving unpresidentially, there are numerous examples of elected officials who have taken a stand against hostile political rhetoric and negative behavior. Former President George W. Bush and several notable senators have consciously made the decision to speak out against divisive language and have denounced the act of bullying and bigotry from the highest levels of leadership in the United States. What remains to be answered is "Where is the line for acceptable and unacceptable behavior?" And, why is it that those individuals who claim to agree with hostile rhetoric only agree when the microaggression is targeted at someone else, but when the tables are turned and a hostile remark is made against them, they claim they are being attacked or unfairly targeted? In essence, they get their feelings hurt. As utopian as it may sound, why not treat others the way you want to be treated? The use of political microaggressions is effective at fostering an atmosphere where regular American citizens and elected officials are apathetic about hostile rhetoric or supporting deprecating views about others, all of which continues to lead to divisiveness and continued inequitable socioeconomic public policies for 99 percent of the population.

# CHAPTER SEVEN

# The Transformation Process and the Challenges Ahead

> Wilders understands that culture and demographics are our destiny.
> We can't restore our civilization with somebody else's babies.[1]

Representative Steve King (R-IA) posted the above statement on Twitter in March 2017. King, a conservative politician known for making controversial remarks, posted his retweet in support of Geert Wilders, the leader of the far-right political party in the Netherlands. Wilders's party ran for office on the platform of immigration reform, calling for an end to immigration from Muslim countries and opposition to the Quran.[2] Wilders is known for his divisive and derogatory remarks toward Muslims; on his Facebook page and in a YouTube video Wilders states, "We Are Being Colonized." "Our Population Is Being Replaced By People With Norms And Values That Are Not Ours."[3] King's tweet supporting a "restoration of civilization" was met with criticism and support. Critics questioned King's nativist endorsement, and supporters such as David Duke, the former grand wizard of the Ku Klux Klan, praised him by tweeting "GOD BLESS STEVE KING!!! #TruthRISING."[4]

Similarly, President Donald Trump is known for stereotyping immigrants from Mexico as illegals, rapists, and "bad hombres." Trump attacked U.S. District Judge Gonzalo Curiel, the presiding judge in litigation against Trump University, claiming Curiel could not be impartial based on his Mexican heritage (Curiel was born in Indiana): "There's a hostility toward me by a judge, tremendous hostility, beyond belief—I believe he happens to be Spanish, which is fine, he's Hispanic, which is fine, and we haven't asked for a recusal, which we may do, but we have a judge who's very hostile."[5] Trump defended his inflammatory comments against Curiel in a televised interview:

**Trump:** I've had horrible rulings, I've been treated very unfairly by this judge. Now this judge is of Mexican heritage. I'm building a wall, ok? I'm building a wall.

**Interviewer:** No Mexican judge could ever be involved in a case that involves you?

**Trump:** Well, nah, he's a member of a society where you know very pro Mexico and that's fine, it's all fine, but I think, I think he should recuse himself.

**Interviewer:** It sounds like you are calling into question his heritage? Because he's Latino?

**Trump:** I think he should recuse himself.

Later in the interview:

**Interviewer:** If you are saying he can't do his job because of his race, is that not the definition of racism?

**Trump:** No, I don't think so at all. No.

**Interviewer:** No?

**Trump:** No, he's proud of his heritage, I respect him for that.

**Interviewer:** Are you saying he can't do his job because of it?

**Trump:** Look, he's proud of his heritage, okay. He's a Mexican, we're building a wall between here and Mexico. . .

**Interviewer:** He's not from Mexico, he's from Indiana.

**Trump:** He's of Mexican heritage and he's very proud of it.[6]

Republicans at all levels denounced Trump for his inflammatory remarks. Paul Ryan (R-WI), current Speaker of the House of Representatives, called Trump's comments "the textbook example of a racist comment;"[7] Newt Gingrich, former Speaker of the House and former U.S. presidential candidate, stated Trump's comments were "inexcusable."[8] Senate Majority Leader Mitch McConnell (R-KY) said "I couldn't disagree more."[9] Coincidently, these elected officials denounced Trump's microaggression and demagogic rhetoric about Judge Curiel but continue to support Trump, as do other elected officials at all levels of government. While I concede that campaigning for the highest office in the United States is not for the fainthearted, do we as citizens have a responsibility to expect more from our elected officials? When did it become acceptable for political elites to "microaggress" themselves into political office? Or is it that the Founding Fathers did such an exceptional job laying the groundwork in their use of microaggressions that it has now become the accepted practice in order to win office? Once elected officials are in office, are citizens responsible for "calling out" those who continue to espouse microaggressive rhetoric that creates another layer of divisiveness in a country that is already socially, economically, and politically stratified?

## Implications of Changing Demographics

The larger implication from the two vignettes above is that demographics are changing, and some elected officials are uncomfortable with the change. Steve King's tweet, "We can't restore our civilization with somebody else's babies," is a microaggression with nativist rationale. King's narrow view of civilization is that only a certain group or population can continue to maintain social, political, and economic values. On the other hand, Trump's comments about Judge Curiel are a combination of a microassault, microinsult, and microinvalidation. Trump holds a biased attitude about Judge Curiel because of his ethnicity; his comment was racist, and he negates a person of color.

Recall from Chapter 1 that political microaggressions are direct, intentional, verbal, and divisive comments that communicate hostile, derogatory, or negative insults toward a person, group, or organization. And, microaggressions take the form of a microassault, microinsult, and microinvalidation. King's tweet and Trump's statements have become standard examples of how microaggressions are acceptable in political rhetoric and used as a weapon to frame individuals, groups, or organizations as degenerate. Trump's statements may be a forewarning of things to come, as a segment of society has embraced his rhetoric and outlook on Latinos and Muslims. At the heart of the "us versus them" debate is a myth, stereotype, and bias that changing demographics will infringe on American values, mores, and traditions. But the real question we should be asking is whose values, mores, and traditions are we ascribing to—the Founding Fathers, who reinforced social, economic, and political stratification? Do we all have to speak one language, eat apple pie, and enjoy the game of baseball to be considered American? Or, can we be multilingual, eat sushi, and enjoy soccer and be considered American? And how do we reconcile the notion of Americanism when microaggressions are reinforced through political rhetoric in order to create divisions of "us versus them"?

Reflectively, we need to question whether Trump's microaggressions are any different from those of Thomas Jefferson, who wrote that blacks were inferior to whites; Benjamin Franklin, who compared Germans to swarming hogs; or Abraham Lincoln stating that he belonged to the superior race in his debate with Stephen A. Douglas. Is it the era in which we now live, with access to 24-hour cable television, the Internet, and mobile devices, that draws attention to the hostile political rhetoric proffered by political elites? Despite being a civilized society, Americans have become tolerant of microaggressions in political rhetoric that under any other circumstances would equate to bullying. Changing demographics have unnerved those who have held social, economic and political power since America's founding, and rhetoric continues to be used as a weapon to suppress those groups who might be shifting the equilibrium. Microaggressions are the central tenet that keep some elected officials in office. Take for example, Greg Gianforte, a multimillionaire Republican candidate for Montana's only seat in the House of Representatives, who in May 2017 assaulted a *Guardian* political reporter for asking a question regarding healthcare. Gianforte was charged with assault and sentenced to community service and anger management classes; nonetheless, he still managed to win the congressional seat.

## A Call to Action

Eliminating microaggressions from political rhetoric will not be an easy task. Elected officials have relied on the use of microaggressions since the nation's founding, and they understand that some in society subscribe to the disparaging and vilification of others. As I have argued in this book, the direct, intentional, verbal, and divisive comments that communicate hostile, derogatory, or negative insults toward a person, group, or organization help those in power justify their views and policies. I have also argued that many perpetrators of microaggressions attack in a conscious and deliberate manner. In essence, they calculate the shock value of denigrating others. Political microaggressions are used to create an environment where certain groups are perceived as inferior and a threat to Americanism (e.g., Native Americans during the founding of the United States, African Americans during the civil rights era, Latinos before and after the Treaty of Guadalupe Hidalgo, and countless other groups). These views reinforce the "us versus them" paranoia and heighten the sense of "group position" in which the dominant group believes it is superior and entitled to certain privileges and rights, while those outside the dominant group want to belong to the preferred status of the dominant group.[10] As such, political microaggressions cannot be easily eliminated from politics because rebutting negative rhetoric and framing has historically had negligible impact. For individuals who approve of using microaggressions to frame others negatively, it is because they already hold hostile preconceived beliefs and attitudes about a person, group, or organization. For these individuals microaggressions solidify their belief that certain groups are inferior and un-American.

Political microaggressions, like all microaggressions, cannot be easily eliminated from formal and informal discourse. As such, the primary objective of this book was to disentangle the constructs of political microaggressions and explain how they are used as a weapon in a changing racial and ethnic environment. As Pierce, Carew, Pierce-Gonzalez, and Wills declared in 1978, microaggressions are rooted in a group's sense of superiority over inferior groups.[11] This line of reasoning is heightened when elected officials at various levels of government communicate hostile rhetoric to citizens. Consider the issue of illegal immigration. Now consider how immigrants are portrayed by some elected officials and the media. The typical elected official frames illegal immigrants as criminals, welfare recipients, and taking jobs from Americans. Now, consider how the media frames the issue of illegal immigration. Often the media will show news footage of suspected undocumented Latino men standing around on street corners or being arrested. Moreover, when the Department of Homeland Security conducts immigration raids, the media typically shows footage of Latinos being arrested. Immigration scholars, activists, and attorneys recognize that only half of the 11.5 million undocumented immigrants in the United States are from Mexico and Central and Latin America. So, why are only Latinos framed as undocumented? Who are the remaining six million undocumented immigrants? Are these subtle yet effective microaggressions engrained deeper in our society than we care to admit?

It would be naïve to argue that the sociopolitical idea of "us versus them" is isolated to one group, race, religion, or political party. The perception of "us versus them" is a dynamic that permeates within every group, race, religion, and political party. As such, a point we should not overlook is that an individual's use of toxic political rhetoric and negative behavior appeals to some within our inner circle who may share our dinner table. This should be enough to make us uncomfortable and provide us the opportunity to speak up and denounce microaggressions and preconceived biased attitudes. We should engage in constructive dialogue when misinformation or inaccurate generalizations create divisions and dissension based on race, religion, political party, or socioeconomic status. As former president George W. Bush stated in his speech at The Spirit of Liberty: At Home, In The World forum:

> Our identity as a nation—unlike many other nations—is not determined by geography or ethnicity, by soil or blood. Being an American involves the embrace of high ideals and civic responsibility. . . . Bullying and prejudice in our public life sets a national tone, provides permission for cruelty and bigotry, and compromises the moral education of children. The only way to pass along civic values is to first live up to them.
>
> Finally, the Call to Action calls on the major institutions of our democracy, public and private, to consciously and urgently attend to the problem of declining trust.[12]

In this concluding chapter, I will offer four suggestions for combating the use of microaggressions in everyday life and minimizing political microaggressions in a changing political and racial environment. I offer these four recommendations as a starting point for moving forward in an atmosphere where microaggression has become the norm. In Chapter 2, I discussed changing demographics from minority to majority and how non-Hispanic whites who have held the majority since the nation's founding are unaccustomed to the changing ethnic balance and political environment precipitated by the growth in minority groups. The chapter argued that demographics matter because changes impact languages spoken, customary cultures, religious observations, and how groups view and interact with each other. Economic and political instruments associated with changing demographics are "often subtle and seemingly nonracial,"[13] but these instruments have much larger implications ranging from political underrepresentation to housing discrimination, voter disenfranchisement, and economic inequality to access to higher education along with numerous other economic, political, and social areas. Nativists advocate for the homogenization of the United States, but the rapid proliferation of Latino and Asian populations will lead to a more heterogenous population.

In Chapter 3, I established that the use of political microaggressions by political elites is not a new phenomenon. Political elites have used political microaggressions throughout the history of the United States to frame a variety of issues and exploit the differences between groups. As is evident from the writings of Abraham Lincoln, Benjamin Franklin, and Thomas Jefferson, some of the most revered Founding Fathers were perpetrators of microaggressions. Though their comments were the popular thought of the era, this does not negate the truth that microaggressions were used to insult and denigrate blacks and slaves. For example, Lincoln in his senatorial debate with Douglas feverously argued against slavery, stating, "I hate it because of the monstrous injustice of slavery itself,"[14] but in that same debate Lincoln also states, "I have no purpose to introduce political and social equality between the white and the black races."[15] Although Lincoln abhorred the institution of slavery, he was also aware of the complexities of repealing slavery and the political implications of suggesting a repeal at that point in time.[16] Fastforward to the 21st century, and political microaggressions are still in use. Recall the case studies of modern-day locally elected commissioners and mayors who have been recipients of microaggressions by colleagues. When non-Hispanic whites are confronted with changing demographics in office, they use microaggressions to frame the "perceived threat" in a negative manner. Many rely on name calling, threats, and racism to validate their superior status. Alternatively, many perpetrators of political microaggressions claim they are simply expressing what everyone else is thinking, and those who reject the insult are considered too politically correct. However, when non-Hispanic whites are directly challenged about their comments, they seemingly backtrack and qualify their statements with "I did not intend to insult" or "We have to pick the right time" to confront perpetrators of microaggressions.

Chapter 4 introduced several theories of nativism and recounted the long history of nativist attitudes against American minority groups. The chapter established that the political rhetoric of 2017 is not new in denigrating specific minority groups. African Americans, Asian Americans, Latinos, Muslims, and other groups have once again become the targets of microaggressions and deliberate negative framing by political elites. In Chapter 5, I discussed the realization that times are changing, and survey data indicates that defining Americanism is a multifaceted endeavor. Language, specifically the ability to speak English, was singled out as important in identifying as American, but being born and having an American ancestry were not as important as far as being considered truly American. Political microaggressions are analogous to Pandora's box; although individuals and political elites use insults and hostile political rhetoric to define the political and social landscape, the effects also provide a platform for nativists, extremists, and hate groups to frame other groups as lower on the hierarchical ladder. It is this framing that perpetrators use to insist they are only saying what everyone else is thinking and doing what everyone wishes they could do. These are important points to consider as demographics continue to change.

Chapter 6 examined the unconventionality of Trump and why some individuals feel that he gets away with using microaggressions. The chapter presented the imperceptive panacea influence (IPI) framework as a way to explain why Trump continues to find support among voters. For some individuals there is an unintentional lack of awareness about certain actions, and others intentionally make a calculated decision to ignore and/or minimize the microaggressive actions of others. For an individual in this second form of IPI, toxic political rhetoric and negative behavior is what attracts them to a candidate. When a candidate or elected official engages in hostile political rhetoric, individuals in this group continue to support the elected official or candidate because hostile rhetoric internally resonates with them.

## What Does This All Mean?

With changing demographics, a sense of superiority is heightened by some in the majority as a way to preserve their status. Changing demographics heighten the use of microaggressions against groups that are seen as infringing on economic, political, and social status that have historically been controlled by the majority. Growing minority groups are met with intentional microaggressions meant to denigrate and minimize their economic, political, and social capital. Is it possible to deconflict nativist rhetoric and changing demographics? More important, do political elites want to deconflict the eventual clash? What does it mean for American values, democracy, and institutions if we as citizens continue to accept the use of microaggressions from political elites? The 2016 U.S. presidential election revealed that, at some level, many in society tolerate the use of political microaggressions—how do we move past these deeply ingrained ideological predispositions that cloud rational thought? As I argued in Chapter 5, the majority of Americans will not follow an intolerant leader, and only a few prefer isolationism and homogeneity. The majority of Americans will rebuff the use of microaggressions and the use of political rhetoric as a weapon. Most Americans are able to conceptualize that "American values," whatever those values may be, will continue to hold strong. For example, recall the survey in Chapter 5, which found that more than 40 percent of respondents indicated that one does not have to be born in the United States to be truly American.[17] And only 29 percent of respondents surveyed thought it was very important to follow American customs and traditions.[18] This seems to indicate that Americans are more tolerant and welcoming of others than we have been led to believe based on the political rhetoric of the most recent presidential election.

Moreover, while a small group of individuals continues to gravitate toward hostile political rhetoric and the use of microaggressions, other individuals have used their high-profile platforms to reject microaggressive behavior and nativist inclinations. Individuals such as former presidents George H.W. Bush, George W. Bush, and Barack Obama; Senators Corker, Flake McCain, and Sasse; Canadian prime minister Justin Trudeau; German chancellor Angela Merkel; French president Emmanuel Macron, and other leaders domestically and internationally have expressed their discontent with divisive and reckless rhetoric. Thus, American values will continue to flourish and hold strong regardless of the rhetoric that permeates this unconventional political era.

## Recommendations

In the following section, I offer four recommendations as a way to move forward in an atmosphere where political rhetoric has become a weapon and microaggression has become normalized.

One, repudiate microaggressions. Take for example how officials elected to local government confronted perpetrators as soon as a microaggression was espoused. Perpetrators of intentional, calculated microaggressions are bullies. One thing bullies do not like is an actual confrontation. Thus, it becomes imperative to stop the "bad behavior" as soon as it surfaces. Bullies are okay using inflammatory rhetoric against others, but when the tables are turned and microaggressions are used against them, then they cry foul.

Two, understand that Samuel Huntington was mistaken when he argued there was only one American dream. The findings from the ANES survey show defining or characterizing an individual as American is a complex process. Moreover, how do we define the American dream? Groups of individuals share common traditions and cultures, but this does not imply that individuals or groups are monolithic. There are variations to traditions and cultures, but these variations do not negate individuals from seeing themselves as American or holding American values, whatever those values may be. The foundation of the United States was created by slaves and immigrants. Slaves were uprooted from their homeland and forced to be laborers for Anglo-Saxons. The Chinese helped build the transcontinental railroad, Mexicans worked in U.S. agriculture during World War II, the Irish were instrumental for their work on the East Coast, and the Germans established schools and commerce in Central Texas and elsewhere. All of these groups identify as American, and they dreamed of America in their own languages. Thus, the central thesis of Huntington's argument is factually incorrect. We need only look at history to refute his argument and other nativist inclinations.

Three, citizens live in de facto segregation and need to make efforts to step outside of their insulated comfort zones and engage in conversations with different people. In other words, whites live in white neighborhoods; African Americans live in African American neighborhoods. Each of these groups only knows what they experience in their immediate space, see on cable television, read on the Internet, and hear from elected officials. While institutional systems have been responsible for some de facto segregation, society as a whole is also responsible for self-segregation. How can citizens expect to empathize with others when they surround themselves with people who are similar to them? For example, it is difficult for a white family who lives in Winnetka, Illinois, and is surrounded by family and friends who live in the same area to understand or empathize about issues that are important to African Americans who live in Englewood or Fuller Park in Chicago. It is also difficult for the Latino family who lives in Brownsville, Texas, to understand or empathize with issues that are important to whites in rural West Texas. This circular argument can apply to all races, ethnicities, income levels, educational levels, political preferences, and so forth. While these examples may seem extreme, the point remains that citizens do not intermingle outside their comfort zones. If citizens continue to isolate themselves from other groups, preconceived stereotypes and attitudes continue, making it difficult to reconcile group differences. The question that remains is, why should citizens want to step outside their comfort zone? While I concede that stepping outside of one's comfort zone is uncomfortable, it is that feeling of uncomfortableness that challenges us and our preconceived notions and ideas that we might hold. When we challenge what we think we know, we realize we might not know what we think we know.

Four, individuals in public service, religious leaders, academics, corporate America, and all other individuals in positions of leadership need to be more engaged in denouncing the use of microaggressions. While politics today is more inclined to rally around political parties instead of constituents, we do not work for elected officials—they work for us. That means constituents get to call them out for actions unbecoming of a public servant. If citizens cannot go to school or work and espouse microaggressions, why should citizens extend that to people who serve us? Recall the speech by Newt Gingrich to college Republicans:

> You don't want to trust politicians, you want to hold them accountable. You want to be able to say to them, "We have a contractual relationship, based on that I am a stockholder for you in your campaign, and if you do not listen to me and do something," I don't mean that they're going to obey you like a puppet, but at least understand where your problems are, "If you're not going to listen to me and honor me, then I'm going to sell my stock in you and I'm going to invest in somebody else and we're going to beat you."[19]

This applies to Republicans, Democrats, and Independents alike. If elected officials refuse to be held accountable, then citizens should sell their stock and reinvest. Part of the solution is holding our elected officials and elites to basic standards of decent interpersonal conduct.

## Closing Thoughts

The objective of this book was not to deprecate or demean any particular racial group or political party. As Eduardo Bonilla-Silva states, "Hunting for racists is the sport of choice for those who practice the clinical approach to race-relations—the careful separation of good and bad, tolerant and intolerant Americans."[20] Instead this book offered a glimpse at the use of political rhetoric as a weapon. Its foundation rests in the use of everyday microaggressions that we have become accustomed and tolerant of—belittling and minimizing individuals or groups that may seem different or inferior to us. At the outset of this book I established that we have all been perpetrators of microaggression in some form or another and at the same time the majority of us have also been victims of microaggressions. The issues and questions this book sought to answer were "Why should we care that microaggressions are used in politics?" and "Does negative political rhetoric really matter?" In an effort to answer this from an analytical perspective, this book provided an examination of how embedded hostile political rhetoric is in our political system.

Although the book offered an analysis of how effective political rhetoric infused with microaggressions is, some individuals may feel uncomfortable with this book. Because microaggressions are about more than just politics, and more important, because microaggressions have impacted us all in one way or another, accounts or episodes in this book may have triggered a conscious or internal response from some readers. Moreover, because some readers may have engaged in microaggressions at higher rates than others, there is very little I can do to ease the discomfort some readers may have experienced. Instead, I encourage those readers who may be uncomfortable with the book to reflect on the impact of their actions and words. While many readers may not have been aware of their use of microaggressions, there also will be those readers who knowingly hold preconceived attitudes about race, religion, or political party. For these readers I encourage you to step outside of your comfort zone and experience the world through another reader's perspective. It could be fascinating or, at the very least, a learning experience.

# Notes

## Introduction

1. Marianne Schnall, "An Interview with Maya Angelou," *Psychology Today*, February 17, 2009, https://www.psychologytoday.com/blog/the-guest -room/200902/interview-maya-angelou.

2. Federal Election Commission, 2016 Presidential Campaign Finance, Compare Candidates. http://classic.fec.gov/disclosurep/pnational.do.

3. Jan Mickelson, "Rep. King Defends, Expands on Comments about 'Our Civilization,'" *Jan Mickelson Show*, 1040 WHO radio (Des Moines, Iowa), January 2017. http://whoradio.iheart.com/onair/mickelson-in-the-morning-7738/rep-king -defends-expands-on-comments-15640864/.

4. Refer to: Arlie Russell Hochschild, *Strangers in Their Own Land: Anger and Mourning on the American Right* (New York: New Press, 2016).

## Chapter 1: Subtle Yet Effective: Microaggression Cues

1. Betsy Woodruff, "Lou Holtz on Immigrant 'Invasion': 'I Don't Want to Become You.'" *Daily Beast*, July 19, 2016, http://www.thedailybeast.com/cheats /2016/07/19/holtz-goes-on-immigrant-bashing-rnc-rant.html?via=desktop&sou rce=copyurl.

2. Chester M. Pierce, Jean V. Carew, Diane Pierce-Gonzalez, and Deborah Wills, "An Experiment in Racism: TV Commercials," *Sage Contemporary, Social Science Issues* 44 (1978): 62–88.

3. Lindsay Perez Huber and Daniel G. Solorzano, "Racial Microaggressions as a Tool for Critical Race Research," *Race Ethnicity and Education* 18, no. 3 (2014): 297–320.

4. Derald Wing Sue, "Microaggressions in Everyday Life," October 4, 2010. https://www.youtube.com/watch?v=BJL2P0JsAS4.

5. Woodruff, "Lou Holtz on Immigrant 'Invasion.'"

6. Derald Wing Sue, *Microaggressions in Everyday Life: Race, Gender, and Sexual Orientation* (Hoboken, NJ: John Wiley and Sons, 2010); Derald Wing Sue, "Microaggressions, Marginality, and Oppression: An Introduction," in *Microaggressions and Marginality: Manifestation, Dynamics, and Impact*, ed. Derald Wing Sue (Hoboken, NJ: John Wiley and Sons, 2010); Derald Wing Sue, Christina M. Capodilupo, Gina C. Torino, Jennifer M. Bucceri, Aisha M.B. Holder, Kevin L. Nadal, and Marta Esquilin, "Racial Microaggressions in Everyday Life: Implications for Clinical Practice," *American Psychologist* 62 (2007): 271–86; Derald Wing Sue, Kevin L. Nadal, Christina M. Capodilupo, Annie I. Lin, Gina C. Torino, and David P. Rivera, "Racial Microaggressions against Black Americans: Implications for Counseling," *Journal of Counseling and Development* 86, no. 3 (2008): 330–38.

7. Sue, *Microaggressions in Everyday Life*; Sue, "Microaggressions, Marginality, and Oppression"; Sue et al., "Racial Microaggressions in Everyday Life."

8. Sue, *Microaggressions in Everyday Life*.

9. Anderson J. Franklin, "Invisibility Syndrome and Racial Identity Development in Psychotherapy and Counseling African American Men," *Counseling Psychologist* 27, no. 6 (1991): 761–93.

10. Madonna G. Constantine and Derald Wing Sue, "Perceptions of Racial Microaggressions among Black Supervisees in Cross-Racial Dyads," *Journal of Counseling Psychology* 54, no. 2 (2007): 142–53.

11. Derald Wing Sue, *Overcoming Our Racism: The Journey to Liberation* (San Francisco: Jossey-Bass, 2003).

12. Madonna G. Constantine, "Racial Microaggressions against African American Clients in Cross-Racial Counseling Relationships." *Journal of Counseling Psychology* 54 (2007): 1–16.

13. Donald J. Trump, (@realDonaldTrump), Twitter, February 5, 2018, https://twitter.com/realdonaldtrump/status/960492998734868480.

14. Sue, *Microaggressions in Everyday Life*.

15. Sue, *Microaggressions in Everyday Life*.

16. Pierce, Carew, Pierce-Gonzalez, and Wills, "An Experiment in Racism"; Sue, *Microaggressions in Everyday Life*; Sue, "Microaggressions in Everyday Life"; Sue, "Microaggressions, Marginality, and Oppression"; Sue et al., "Racial Microaggressions in Everyday Life."

17. Derald Wing Sue discusses marginality and oppression from the use of microaggressions. While Sue does not state that political rhetoric causes marginalization and oppressions, the implications of microaggressions in regard to political rhetoric are the same. Negative or hostile political rhetoric marginalizes certain groups and pushes these groups out of mainstream economic, political, and social systems. See Sue, "Microaggressions, Marginality, and Oppression," 5–7.

18. Sue, *Microaggressions in Everyday Life*; Sue, "Microaggressions, Marginality, and Oppression."

19. Sue, "Microaggressions, Marginality, and Oppression."

20. Sue, *Microaggressions in Everyday Life*.

21. Bill Morlin, "Anti-Immigrant Hate Slurs Lead to Fatal Shooting in Kansas," *Hatewatch*, February 24, 2017, https://www.splcenter.org/hatewatch/2017/02/24/anti-immigrant-hate-slurs-lead-fatal-shooting-kansas.

22. Sue, *Microaggressions in Everyday Life*; Sue, "Microaggressions, Marginality, and Oppression."

23. Jordon Fabian, "5 Politicians Who Made Racist Remarks," *ABC News*, March 29, 2013, http://abcnews.go.com/ABC_Univision/Politics/politicians-made-racist-remarks/story?id=18841740#2.

24. Sue, *Microaggressions in Everyday Life*; Sue, "Microaggressions, Marginality, and Oppression."

25. Sue, *Microaggressions in Everyday Life*.

26. Sue, "Microaggressions, Marginality, and Oppression."

27. Tara J. Yosso, William A. Smith, Miguel Ceja, and Daniel G. Solorzano, "Critical Race Theory, Racial Microaggressions, and Campus Racial Climate for Latina/o Undergraduates," *Harvard Educational Review* 79, no. 4 (2009): 659–90.

28. Daniel Solorzano, Miguel Ceja, and Tara Tosso, "Critical Race Theory, Racial Microaggressions, and Campus Racial Climate: The Experiences of African American College Students," *Journal of Negro Education* 69, no. 1/2 (Winter–Spring 2000): 60–73; Valerie Purdie-Vaughns, Claude M. Steele, Paul G. Davies, Ruth Diltmann, and Jennifer Randall Crosby, "Social Identity Contingencies: How Diversity Cues Signal Threat or Safety for African Americans in Mainstream Institutions," *Journal of Personality and Social Psychology* 94, no. 4 (2008): 615–30.

29. Lee Anne Bell, "Sincere Fictions: The Pedagogical Challenges of Preparing White Teachers for Multicultural Classrooms," *Equity and Excellence in Education* 35 (2002): 236–44; Sue, "Microaggressions in Everyday Life."

30. Ayana Allen, Lakia M. Scott, and Chance W. Lewis, "Racial Microaggressions and African American and Hispanic Students in Urban Schools: A Call for Culturally Affirming Education," *Interdisciplinary Journal of Teaching and Learning* 3, no. 2 (2013): 117–29.

31. Quaylan Allen, "They Think Minority Means Lesser Than: Black Middle-Class Sons and Fathers Resisting Microaggressions in the School," *Urban Education* 48, no. 2 (2012): 171–97.

32. See Paul Felix Lazarsfeld, Bernard Berelson, and Hazel Gaudet, *The People's Choice: How the Voter Makes Up His Mind in a Presidential Campaign* (New York: Columbia University Press, 1948); Bernard R. Berelson, Paul F. Lazarsfeld, and William N. McPhee, *Voting: A Study of Opinion Formation in a Presidential Campaign* (Chicago: University of Chicago, 1954); Donald D. Searing, Joel J. Schwartz, and Alden E. Lind, "The Structuring Principle: Political Socialization and Belief Systems," *American Political Science Review* 67, no. 2 (1973): 415–32; Donald D. Searing, Gerald Wright, and George Rabinowitz, "The Primacy Principle: Attitude Change and Political Socialization." *British Journal of Political Science* 6, no. 1 (1976): 83–113; Peter K. Hatemi, Carolyn L. Funk, Sarah E. Medland, Hermine M. Maes, Judy L. Silberg, Nicholas G. Martin, and Lindon J. Eaves, "Genetic and Environmental Transmission of Political Attitudes over a

Life Time," *Journal of Politics* 71, no. 3 (2009): 1141–56; M. Kent Jennings, Laura Stoker, and Jake Bowers, "Politics across Generations: Family Transmission Reexamined," *Journal of Politics* 71, no. 3 (2009): 782–99.

33. Derald Wing Sue, Annie I. Lin, Gina C. Torino, Christina M. Capodilupo, and David P. Rivera, "Racial Microaggressions and Difficult Dialogues on Race in the Classroom," *Cultural Diversity and Ethnic Minority Psychology* 15, no. 2 (2009): 183–90.

34. This account was disclosed in an interview session with subject.

35. This account was disclosed in an interview session with subject.

36. Microinvalidations are often unconscious and occur outside the awareness of a perpetrator. Sue, *Microaggressions in Everyday Life*; Sue, "Microaggressions, Marginality, and Oppression."

37. Numerous studies find that when an individual from an underrepresented group is promoted to a position of authority or leadership, the individual is subjected to a higher standard and scrutiny from the majority group. Refer to Rosabeth Moss Kanter, "Some Effects of Proportions on Group Life: Skewed Sex Ratios and Responses to Token Women," *American Journal of Sociology* 82 (1977): 965–90; Adia Harvey Wingfield and John Harvey Wingfield, "When Visibility Hurts and Helps: How Intersections of Race and Gender Shape Black Professional Men's Experiences with Tokenization," *Cultural Diversity and Ethnic Minority Psychology* 20, no. 4 (2014): 483–90.

38. Sue, *Microaggressions in Everyday Life*.

39. Microaggressions are brief and commonplace verbal, behavioral, and environmental insults (Sue et al. "Racial Microaggressions in Everyday Life") that are often ambiguous and subtle. Bashford, Offermann, and Behrend examine the workplace gender microaggressions (see Tessa E. Bashford, Lynn R. Offermann, and Tara S. Behrend, "Do You See What I See? Perceptions of Gender Microaggressions in the Workplace," *Psychology of Women Quarterly* 38, no. 3 (2014): 340–49).

40. For a discussion on superior and inferior orientation, refer to: Donald G. Gardner and Jon L. Pierce, "A Question of False Self-Esteem: Organization-Based Self-Esteem and Narcissism in Organizational Contexts," *Journal of Managerial Psychology* 26, no. 8 (2011): 682–99; Justin Kruger and David Dunning, "Unskilled and Unaware of It: How Difficulties in Recognizing One's Own Incompetence Lead to Inflated Self Assessments," *Journal of Personality and Social Psychology* 77, no. 6 (1999): 1121–34; Felicia Pratto, Jim Sidanius, Lisa M. Stallworth, and Bertram F. Malle, "Social Dominance Orientation: A Personality Variable Predicting Social and Political Attitudes," *Journal of Personality and Social Psychology* 67, no. 4 (1994): 741–63; Valerie Tiberius and John D. Walker, "Arrogance," *American Philosophical Quarterly* 35, no. 4 (1998): 379–90.

41. Christina M. Capodilupo, Kevin L. Nadal, Lindsay Corman, Sahran Hamit, Oliver B. Lyons, and Alexa Weinberg, "The Manifestations of Gender Microaggressions," in *Microaggressions and Marginality: Manifestation, Dynamics, and Impact*, ed. Derald Wing Sue (Hoboken, NJ: John Wiley and Sons, 2010).

42. Franklin, "Invisibility Syndrome and Racial Identity Development."

43. Constantine and Sue, "Perceptions of Racial Microaggressions."

44. Constantine and Sue, "Perceptions of Racial Microaggressions," 146.

45. Because microaggressions are cumulative, the damaging effects from microaggressions vary from continued stereotypic views (Solorzano, Ceja, and Yosso, "Critical Race Theory"), to cues that suggest certain social group identities are less worthy (Purdie-Vaughns et al, "Social Identity Contingencies").

46. Sue et al., "Racial Microaggressions in Everyday Life."

47. Sue, *Microaggressions in Everyday Life*.

48. Michele Richinick, "South Carolina Dem Chair Bashes Governor: Nikki Haley Is a 'Fraud,'" *NBC News*, May 7, 2013, http://www.nbcnews.com/id/5180 6637/t/south-carolina-dem-chair-bashes-governor-nikki-haley-fraud/#.WMISc DvyuUk.

49. Richinick, "South Carolina Dem Chair Bashes Governor."

50. This account was disclosed in an interview session with subject.

51. Domenico Montanaro, "Hillary Clinton's Basket of Deplorables, In Full Context of This Ugly Campaign," NPR, September 10, 2016, http://www.npr .org/2016/09/10/493427601/hillary-clintons-basket-of-deplorables-in-full -context-of-this-ugly-campaign.

52. Arlie Russell Hochschild, *Strangers in Their Own Land: Anger and Mourning on the American Right* (New York: New Press, 2016).

53. Jerome Rabow, Pauline Venieris, and Manpreet Dhillon, *Ending Racism in America: One Microaggression at a Time* (Dubuque, IA: Kendall Hunt, 2014).

54. William A. Gamson and Andre Modigliani, "The Changing Culture of Affirmative Action," in *Research in Political Sociology*, vol. 3, ed. Richard D. Braungart (Greenwich, CT: JAI, 1987), 143.

55. Robert M. Entman, "Framing: Toward Clarification of a Fractured Paradigm," *Journal of Communication* 43 (1993): 51–58.

56. Entman, "Framing."

57. James N. Druckman, "The Implications of Framing Effects for Citizen Competence," *Political Behavior* 23, no. 3 (2001): 225–56.

58. See Shanto Iyengar, *Is Anyone Responsible? How Television Frames Political Issues* (Chicago: University of Chicago Press, 1991); D.M. McLeod and B.H. Detenber, "Framing Effects of Television News Coverage of Social Protest," *Journal of Communication* 49. no. 3 (2006): 3–23; Thomas E. Nelson, Rosalee A. Clawson, and Zoe M. Oxley, "Media Framing of a Civil Liberties Conflict and Its Effect on Tolerance," *American Political Science Review* 91, no. 3 (1997): 567–83.

59. Thomas E. Nelson and Donald R. Kinder, "Issue Frames and Group-Centrism in American Public Opinion," *Journal of Politics* 58, no. 4 (1996): 1055–78.

60. Nelson and Kinder, "Issue Frames and Group-Centrism," 1058.

61. Sam R. Hall, "Were Thompson's Remarks in 'Best Interest of Humanity'?" *Clarion-Ledger*, April 30, 2014, http://www.clarionledger.com/story/dailyledes /2014/04/30/bennie-thompson-radio-remarks-racist-or-best-interest-humanity /8511131/.

62. Hall, "Thompson's Remarks."

63. W. Lance Bennett and Shanto Iyengar, "A New Era of Minimal Effects? The Changing Foundations of Political Communication," *Journal of Communication* 58, no. 4 (2009): 707–31.

64. Scholars have also examined the effects of agenda setting and priming.

65. See Bernard C. Cohen, *The Press and Foreign Policy* (Princeton, NJ: Princeton University Press, 1963).

66. See the Declaration of Independence, July 4, 1776: "He has excited domestic insurrections amongst us, and has endeavoured to bring on the inhabitants of our frontiers, the merciless Indian Savages, whose known rule of warfare is an undistinguished destruction of all ages, sexes and conditions."

67. For a discussion on partisanship and/or partisan sorting, see Angus Campbell, Philip E. Converse, Warren E. Miller, and Donald E. Stokes, *The American Voter* (New York: John Wiley & Sons, 1960); Donald Green, Bradley Palmquist, and Eric Schickler, *Partisan Hearts and Minds* (New Haven, CT: Yale University Press, 2002); Steven Green, "Understanding Party Identification: A Social Identity Approach," *Political Psychology* 20, no. 2 (1999): 393–403; Steven Green, "Social Identity Theory and Party Identification," *Social Science Quarterly* 85, no. 1 (2004): 138–53.

68. Refer to Sabine Otten and Dirk Wentura, "About the Impact of Automaticity in the Minimal Group Paradigm: Evidence from Affective Priming Tasks," *European Journal of Social Psychology* 29, no. 8 (1999): 1–23.

69. Michael S. Lewis-Beck, William G. Jacoby, Helmut Norpoth, and Herbert F. Welsberg, *The American Voter Revisited* (Ann Arbor: University of Michigan Press, 2001).

70. Campbell, et al., *The American Voter.*

71. Hubert M. Blalock Jr., *Toward a Theory of Minority-Group Relations* (New York: John Wiley & Sons, 1967). See the discussion on group threat theory, pp. 190–97.

## Chapter 2: Changing Demographics: From Minority to Majority

1. Jeremy Schwartz and Dan Hill, "Silent Majority," *Austin American-Statesman*, October 21, 2016, http://projects.statesman.com/news/latino-representation/.

2. 1980 Census of Population, Characteristics of the Population: General Population Characteristics, Texas, PC80–1-B45 Tex.

3. Derald Wing Sue, *Microaggressions in Everyday Life: Race, Gender, and Sexual Orientation* (Hoboken, NJ: John Wiley and Sons, 2010); Derald Wing Sue, "Microaggressions, Marginality, and Oppression: An Introduction," in *Microaggressions and Marginality: Manifestation, Dynamics, and Impact*, ed. Derald Wing Sue (Hoboken, NJ: John Wiley and Sons, 2010).

4. U.S. Census Bureau, Population Division. 2016. Table 1. Annual Estimates of the Resident Population for the United States, Regions, States, and Puerto Rico: April 1, 2010 to July 1, 2016 (NST-EST2016–01), https://www.census.gov/data/tables/2016/demo/popest/nation-total.html.

5. Sandra L. Colby and Jennifer M. Ortman, *Projections of the Size and Composition of the U.S. Population: 2014 to 2060* (Washington, DC: U.S. Census Bureau, 2014).

6. Colby and Ortman, *Projections.*

7. Colby and Ortman, *Projections.*

8. Karen R. Humes, Nicolas A. Jones, and Roberto R. Ramirez, *Overview of Race and Hispanic Origin: 2010* (Washington DC: U.S. Census Bureau, 2011), https://www.census.gov/prod/cen2010/briefs/c2010br-02.pdf.

9. Richard Alba, "The Likely Persistence of a White Majority: How Census Bureau Statistics Have Misled Thinking about the American Future," *American Prospect*, July 11, 2016, http://prospect.org/article/likely-persistence-white-majority-0. Alba, a professor of sociology at City University of New York, makes the case that the new minority is a myth, citing flaws with how the census captures demographic information, especially data regarding children born to multiracial parents. Alba argues that multiracial children should not be considered minority if they have a white parent, as those children may identify as white. Alba maintains that the issue is with the binary method in which the census categorizes individuals.

10. Elizabeth M. Hoeffel, Sonya Rastogi, Myoung Ouk Kim, and Hasan Shahid, *The Asian Population: 2010* (Washington, DC: U.S. Census Bureau, 2012). As part of federal statistics and administrative reporting, the Office of Management and Budget defines "Asian" as any person having origins in any of the original peoples of the Far East, Southeast Asia, or the Indian subcontinent, including, for example, Cambodia, China, India, Japan, Korea, Malaysia, Pakistan, the Philippine Islands, Thailand, and Vietnam; see *Standards for the Classification of Federal Data on Race and Ethnicity*, https://www.whitehouse.gov/wp-content/uploads/2017/11/fedreg_race-ethnicity.pdf.

11. *Census 2000 Redistricting (Public Law 94–171) Summary File* (Washington, DC: U.S. Census Bureau, 2011), Table PL1 and PL2; and *2010 Census Redistricting Data (Public Law 94–171) Summary File* (Washington, DC: U.S. Census Bureau, 2011), Table P1.

12. *Census 2000 Redistricting*, Table PL1 and PL2; *2010 Census Summary File 1* (Washington, DC: U.S. Census Bureau, 2012). As part of federal statistics and administrative reporting, the Office of Management and Budget defines "Hispanic" or Latino as a person of Mexican, Puerto Rican, Cuban, Central or South American, or other Spanish culture or origin, regardless of race. See *Standards for the Classification of Federal Data on Race and Ethnicity*, https://www.whitehouse.gov/wp-content/uploads/2017/11/fedreg_race-ethnicity.pdf. For the purposes of this project, the terms *Hispanic* and *Latino* are used interchangeably to refer to those populations of Mexican, Puerto Rican, Cuban, Central or South American, or other Spanish culture or origin, regardless of race.

13. U.S. Census Bureau, Census 2000 Summary File 1, https://www.census.gov/census2000/sumfile1.html; *2010 Census Summary File 1*; *Census 2000 Redistricting*, Table PL1 and PL2; *2010 Census Summary File 1* .

14. Michael Hoefer, Nancy Rytina, and Bryan C. Baker, *Estimates of the Unauthorized Immigrant Population Residing in the United States: January 2007* (Washington, DC: Office of Immigration Statistics, 2008); Michael Hoefer, Nancy Rytina and Bryan C. Baker, *Estimates of the Unauthorized Immigrant Population Residing in the United States: January 2008* (Washington, DC: Office of Immigration Statistics, 2009); Michael Hoefer, Nancy Rytina and Bryan C. Baker, *Estimates of the Unauthorized Immigrant Population Residing in the United States: January 2009* (Washington, DC: Office of Immigration Statistics, 2010).

15. V. O. Key in *Southern Politics in State and Nation* (New York: Knopf, 1949) argued that white anger and hostility directed at African Americans was directly based on the size of the African American community. This assessment of group threat should also hold as the size of the Latino population continues to increase.

16. Francine J. Lipman, "Bearing Witness to Economic Injustices of Undocumented Immigrant Families: A New Class of 'Undeserving' Working Poor," *Nevada Law Journal* 7, no. 3 (Summer 2007): 736–58.

17. Stephen H. Legomsky, "Fear and Loathing in Congress and the Courts: Immigration and Judicial Review," *Texas Law Review* 78 (2002): 1615–32.

18. Robert M. Entman, "Framing: Toward Clarification of a Fractured Paradigm," *Journal of Communication* 43 (1993): 51–58.

19. Thomas E. Nelson and Donald R. Kinder, "Issue Frames and Group-Centrism in American Public Opinion," *Journal of Politics* 58, no. 4 (1996): 1055–78.

20. Domenico Montanaro, Danielle Kurtzleben, Scott Horsley, Sarah McCammon, and Richard Gonzales, "Fact Check: Donald Trump's Speech on Immigration," *National Public Radio*, August 31, 2016, http://www.npr.org/2016/08/31/492096565/fact-check-donald-trumps-speech-on-immigration.

21. Howard Zinn, *A People's History of The United States 1492–Present* (New York: Harper Perennial Modern Classics, 2003), 89.

22. Charles A. Beard, *An Economic Interpretation of the Constitution of the United States* (New York: Macmillan, 1921), 25.

23. Beard, *Economic Interpretation*, 25, 325.

24. Joe R. Feagin, *Racist America Roots, Current realities, and Future Reparations*, 3rd ed. (New York: Routledge, 2014).

25. Lisa Garcia Bedolla, *Latino Politics*, 2nd ed. (Malden, MA: Polity, 2014).

26. Jorge M. Chavez and Doris Marie Provine, "Race and the Response of State Legislatures to Unauthorized Immigrants," *Annals of the American Academy of Political and Social Science* 623, no. 78 (2009): 78–92.

27. Chavez and Provine, "Race and the Response of State Legislatures."

28. Ted Brader, Nicholas A. Valentino, and Elizabeth Suhay, "What Triggers Public Opposition to Immigration? Anxiety, Group Cues, and Immigration Threat," *American Journal of Political Science* 52, no. 4 (2008): 959–78.

29. Brader, Valentino, and Suhay, "What Triggers Public Opposition to Immigration?"

30. Samuel P. Huntington, "The Hispanic Challenge," *Foreign Policy*, March/April 2004.

31. For an extensive discussion on minority entry in political, economic, and social spheres, see Martin Gilens and Benjamin I. Page, "Testing Theories of American Politics: Elites, Interest Groups, and Average Citizens," *Perspectives on Politics* 12, no. 3 (2014): 564–81; James R. Kleugel and Eliot R. Smith, *Beliefs about Inequality: Americans' Views of What Is and What Ought to Be* (London: Routledge, 2017).

32. See Stephanie A. Bohn and Meghan Conley, *Immigration and Population* (Cambridge: Polity, 2015).

33. In May 2017, the U.S. Supreme Court refused to restore a stringent North Carolina voting law that was found unconstitutional by a federal appeals court. The North Carolina voting law targeted African Americans by rejecting the forms of identification disproportionality used by African American voters, including IDs issued to government employees, student IDs, and people receiving public assistance. See Adam Liptak and Michael Wines, "Strict North Carolina Voter ID Law Thwarted after Supreme Court Rejects Case," *New York Times*, May 15, 2017, https://www.nytimes.com/2017/05/15/us/politics/voter-id-laws-supreme-court -north-carolina.html?_r=0.

34. For voting patterns in presidential elections by race and Hispanic origin, refer to U.S. Census Historical Reported Voting Rates, Table A-6. Reported Voting and Registration for Total Citizen Voting Age Population, by Race and Hispanic Origin: Presidential Elections 1980–2016.

35. "Elections 2016: Exit Polls," CNN, November 23, 2016, http://www.cnn .com/election/results/exit-polls.

36. "Election Center: President: Full Results," December 10, 2012, http://www .cnn.com/election/2012/results/race/president/.

37. Nicolás C. Vaca, *The Presumed Alliance: The Unspoken Conflict between Latinos and Blacks and What It Means for America* (New York: Rayo, 2004).

38. Matt Barreto and Gary M. Segura, *Latino America: How America's Most Dynamic Population Is Poised to Transform the Politics of the Nation* (New York: Public Affairs, 2014).

39. Martin Guevara Urbina, Joel E. Vela, and Juan O. Sanchez, *Ethnic Realities of Mexican Americans: From Colonialism to 21st Century Globalization* (Springfield, IL: Charles C. Thomas, 2014).

40. Vaca, *Presumed Alliance*.

41. Vaca, *Presumed Alliance*, 1–2.

42. Vaca, *Presumed Alliance*, 2.

43. Feagin, *Racist America* .

44. Feagin, *Racist America*.

45. Mickelson, Jan. 2017. Jan Mickelson with Representative Steve King. "The Jan Mickelson Show on 1040 WHO radio in Des Moines, Iowa. http://whoradio .iheart.com/onair/mickelson-in-the-morning-7738/rep-king-defends-expands -on-comments-15640864/.

46. See Eduardo Bonilla-Silva, *Racism without Racists*, 4th ed. (New York: Rowman & Littlefield, 2014).

47. Donald J. Trump (@realDonaldTrump), Twitter, June 4, 2016, https://twitter .com/realdonaldtrump/status/739080401747120128?lang=en.

48. Donald J. Trump (@realDonaldTrump), Twitter, May 5, 2016, https://twitter .com/realDonaldTrump/status/728297587418247168.

49. Chuck Todd, Sally Bronston, and Matt Rivera, "Rep. John Lewis: 'I Don't See Trump as a Legitimate President,'" *Meet the Press*, January 14, 2017. http:// www.nbcnews.com/meet-the-press/john-lewis-trump-won-t-be-legitimate -president-n706676. Representative John Lewis (D-GA) in a Sunday morning television interview with Chuck Todd of *Meet the Press* argued that Trump was not a legitimate president. When pressed to expand on his comment, Lewis argued that he believed the Russians helped Trump win the election, calling it unfair to the democratic process.

50. Feagin, *Racist America*, 13.

51. See Key, *Southern Politics*.

52. See Donald Bogle, *Toms, Coons, Mulattoes, Mammies, and Bucks: An Interpretive History of Blacks in American Films* (New York: Continuum, 2001); Travis L. Dixon, "Skin Tone, Crime News, and Social Reality Judgments: Priming the Stereotype of the Dark and Dangerous Black Criminal," *Journal of Applied Social Psychology* 35, no. 8 (2005): 1555–70. Subtle media cues have been found to influence racial views about minorities. When cued with stereotypic information about certain groups, audiences will hold negative views about the stereotyped group. See Srividya Ramasubramanian, "The Impact of Stereotypical Versus Counterstereotypical Media Exemplars on Racial Attitudes, Causal Attributions, and Support for Affirmative Action," *Communication Research* 38, no. 4 (2011): 497–516; Linus Abraham and Osei Appiah, "Framing News Stories: The Role of Visual Imagery in Priming Racial Stereotypes," *Howard Journal of Communications* 17, no. 3 (2006): 183–203.

53. Refer to Rosalind S. Chou and Joe R. Feagin, *The Myth of the Model Minority: Asian Americans Facing Racism* (New York: Paradigm, 2015); John Tawa, Karen L. Suyemoto, and Jesse J. Tauriac, "Triangulated Threat: A Model of Black and Asian Race Relations in a Context of White Dominance," in *American Multicultural Studies Diversity of Race, Ethnicity, Gender and Sexuality*, ed. Sherrow O. Pinder (Los Angeles: Sage, 2013), 229–47.

54. "Race Relations," Gallup, http://www.gallup.com/poll/1687/race-relations .aspx.

55. Feagin, *Racist America*, 64.

56. "Race Relations," Gallup, http://www.gallup.com/poll/1687/race-relations .aspx.

57. Arlie Russell Hochschild, *Strangers in Their Own Land: Anger and Mourning on the American Right* (New York: New Press, 2018).

58. For a discussion on majority groups and their opposition to institutional changes, see George Eaton Simpson and J. Milton Yinger, *Racial and Cultural Minorities: An Analysis of Prejudice and Discrimination* (New York: Springer, 1985).

59. "African Americans in Missouri are 75 percent more likely to be stopped and searched by law enforcement officers than Caucasians, are unconscionable, and are simply unacceptable in a progressive society. . . . We share the alarm and concern that black individuals enjoying the highways, roads and points of interest there may not be safe, and the national office will also be closely monitoring the progress of Governor Greitien's review of Bill SB 43." "Travel Advisory for the State of Missouri," NAACP, August 2, 2017, http://www.naacp.org/latest/travel-advisory-state-missouri/.

60. "Travel Advisory for the State of Missouri."

61. Office of the Missouri Attorney General, "2016 Vehicle Stops Executive Summary," https://ago.mo.gov/home/vehicle-stops-report/2016-executive-summary#summary.

62. Office of the Missouri Attorney General, "2016 Vehicle Stops Executive Summary."

63. "ACLU Issues Texas 'Travel Advisory,'" American Civil Liberties Union, https://www.aclu.org/news/aclu-issues-texas-travel-advisory.

64. Southern Poverty Law Center, *Intelligence Report: The Year in Hate and Extremism* (Montgomery, AL: Southern Poverty Law Center, 2017).

65. Southern Poverty Law Center, *Intelligence Report.*

66. Southern Poverty Law Center, *Intelligence Report.*

67. Jessie Daniels, *White Lies: Race, Class, Gender, and Sexuality in White Supremacist Discourse* (New York: Routledge, 1997).

68. For a discussing on why hate groups increase and the determinants that create action, see Rachel M. Duroso and David Jacobs, "The Determinants of the Number of White Supremacist Groups: A Pooled Time-Series Analysis," *Social Problems* 60, no. 1 (2013): 128–44.

69. CNN, "David Duke Praises President Trump at White Supremacist Rally Protest in Charlottesville, Virginia," August 12, 2017, https://www.youtube.com/watch?v=vJ_iezh9vjE.

70. Although Donald Trump denounced the actions of white supremacists, it took two days after the death of Heather Heyer, a counterprotestor participant in Charlottesville, for the president under increasing pressure from fellow Republicans to issue a statement specifically condemning the Ku Klux Klan, white supremacists, and neo-Nazis groups.

71. David Duke, (@DrDavidDuke), Twitter August 12, 2017, https://twitter.com/DrDavidDuke/status/896431991821926401.

72. David Duke (@DrDavidDuke), Twitter, August 14, 2017, https://twitter.com/DrDavidDuke/status/897089950570737664.

73. David Duke (@DrDavidDuke), Twitter, August 14, 2017, https://twitter.com/DrDavidDuke/status/897087595938709504.

74. C-SPAN, "President Trump News Conference," August 15, 2017, https://www.c-span.org/video/?432633–1/president-trump-there-blame-sides-violence-charlottesville.

75. Huntington, "The Hispanic Challenge."

## Chapter 3: Political Discourse: Inflammatory Innuendos

1. Francesca Gillet, "London Bridge Terror Attack: Timeline of Events and How the Horror Unfolded," *Evening Standard*, June 4, 2017. https://www.standard.co.uk/news/london/london-bridge-terror-attack-timeline-of-events-and-how-the-horror-unfolded-a3556371.html.

2. Donald. J. Trump (@realDonaldTrump), Twitter, June 4, 2017. https://twitter.com/realDonaldTrump/status/871325606901895168.

3. See Caitlin Gibson, "How 'Politically Correct' Went from Compliment to Insult," *Washington Post*, January 13, 2016, https://www.washingtonpost.com/lifestyle/style/how-politically-correct-went-from-compliment-to-insult/2016/01/13/b1cf5918-b61a-11e5-a76a-0b5145e8679a_story.html?utm_term=.54a03c6fd09a.

4. Sally Schwartz, *A Mixed Multitude: The Struggle for Toleration in Colonial Pennsylvania* (New York: New York University Press, 1988). For further insight into Penn and his effectiveness at creating a diverse society, see John A. Moretta, *William Penn and the Quaker Legacy* (New York: Pearson Longman, 2007).

5. Edmund S. Morgan, *Benjamin Franklin* (New Haven, CT: Yale University Press, 2002).

6. Benjamin Franklin, *Observations Concerning the Increase of Mankind, the Peopling of Countries, etc.* (New York: William Abbatt, 1918), 10.

7. Benjamin Franklin, *Observations Concerning the Increase of Mankind, the Peopling of Countries, etc.* (New York: William Abbatt, 1918), 224.

8. Dumas Malone, *Jefferson and the Ordeal of Liberty* (Boston: Little, Brown and Company, 1962).

9. Thomas Jefferson, *Notes of the State of Virginia* (New York: Harper & Row, 1964).

10. Jefferson, *Notes of the State of Virginia*.

11. Jefferson, *Notes of the State of Virginia*, 134.

12. Jefferson, *Notes of the State of Virginia*, 138.

13. Howard Jones, *Abraham Lincoln and a New Birth of Freedom: The Union and Slavery in the Diplomacy of the Civil War* (Lincoln: University of Nebraska Press, 1999).

14. Michael Vorenberg, *Final Freedom: The Civil War, the Abolition of Slavery, and the Thirteenth Amendment* (New York: Cambridge University Press, 2001).

15. Rodney O. Davis and Douglas L. Wilson, eds., *The Lincoln-Douglas Debates* (Galesburg, Il: Knox College Lincoln Studies Center; Urbana: University of Illinois Press, 2008), 8–9.

16. James McPherson, *Battle Cry of Freedom: The Civil War Era* (New York: Oxford University Press, 1988).

17. Davis and Wilson, *Lincoln-Douglas Debates*.

18. Davis and Wilson, *Lincoln-Douglas Debates*, 23.

19. Davis and Wilson, *Lincoln-Douglas Debates*, 26.

20. Davis and Wilson, *Lincoln-Douglas Debates*, 27 and 30.

21. Jerome Rabow, Pauline Y. Venieris, and Manpreet Dhillon, *Ending Racism in America One Microaggression at a Time* (Dubuque, IA: Kendall Hunt, 2014).

22. All individuals participated in the interviews voluntarily, and names are confidential. As such, each individual was assigned an indirect identifier.

23. Eduardo Bonilla-Silva, *Racism without Racists*, 4th ed. (New York: Rowman & Littlefield, 2014), 76.

24. Derald Wing Sue, *Microaggressions in Everyday Life: Race, Gender, and Sexual Orientation* (Hoboken, NJ: John Wiley and Sons, 2010); Derald Wing Sue, "Microaggressions, Marginality, and Oppression: An Introduction," in *Microaggressions and Marginality: Manifestation, Dynamics, and Impact*, ed. Derald Wing Sue (Hoboken, NJ: John Wiley and Sons, 2010).

25. Sue, *Microaggressions in Everyday Life*; Sue, "Microaggressions, Marginality, and Oppression."

26. Sue, "Microaggressions, Marginality, and Oppression," 5.

27. Microaggressions are brief and commonplace verbal, behavioral, and environmental insults that impact victims in various psychological ways. See Sue, *Microaggressions in Everyday Life*, 42.

28. Also see Bonilla-Silva, *Racism without Racists*; Joe R. Feagin, *Racist America: Roots, Current Realities, and Future Reparations*, 3rd ed. (New York: Routledge, 2014).

29. Sue, *Microaggressions in Everyday Life*, 52.

30. Sue, *Microaggressions in Everyday Life*; Sue, "Microaggressions, Marginality, and Oppression."

31. Sue, "Microaggressions, Marginality, and Oppression."

## Chapter 4: Nativist Attitudes: American Minority Groups as Targets

1. Alan Blinder and Kevin Sack, "Dylann Roof Is Sentenced to Death in Charleston Church Massacre," *New York Times*, January 10, 2017.

2. Scott Smith, Scott, "Fresno Shooter Wanted to Kill Many White People, Police Say," Associated Press, April 19, 2017.

3. Joe R. Feagin, 2014. *Racist America: Roots, Current Realities, and Future Reparations*, 3rd ed. (New York: Routledge, 2014), 64.

4. Feagin, *Racist America*, 6–7.

5. Feagin, *Racist America*, 6.

6. Clarence Lusane, *The Black History of the White House* (San Francisco: City Lights Books, 2011).

7. Gleaves Whitney, "Slaveholding Presidents," Hauenstein Center for Presidential Studies, July 19, 2006, https://scholarworks.gvsu.edu/ask_gleaves/30.

8. Ronald Takkai, *Iron Cages: Race and Culture in 19th-Century America*, rev ed. (New York: Oxford University Press, 2000).

9. Ryan D. King and Darren Wheelock, "Group Threat and Social Control: Race, Perceptions of Minorities and the Desire to Punish," *Social Forces* 85, no. 3 (2007): 1255–80.

10. Ken Gonzales-Day, *Lynching in the West: 1850–1935* (Durham, NC: Duke University Press, 2006).

11. Carolyn Petrosino, "Connecting the Past to the Future: Hate Crime in America," *Journal of Contemporary Criminal Justice* 15, no. 1 (1999): 22–47.

12. U.S. Department of Justice, Federal Bureau of Investigation, "Civil Rights: Hate Crimes: Defining a Hate Crime," https://www.fbi.gov/investigate/civil-rights /hate-crimes.

13. U.S. Department of Justice, Federal Bureau of Investigation, *Hate Crime Statistics Uniform Crime Reports* (Clarksburg, WV: Department of Justice, 2008).

14. U.S. Department of Justice, Federal Bureau of Investigation, *Hate Crime Statistics Uniform Crime Reports* (Clarksburg, WV: Department of Justice, 2008).

15. William B. Rubenstein, "The Real Story of U.S. Hate Crime Statistics: An Empirical Analysis," *Tulane Law Review* 78 (2004): 1213–46.

16. Rubenstein, "The Real Story of U.S. Hate Crime Statistics."

17. Rubenstein, "The Real Story of U.S. Hate Crime Statistics."

18. U.S. Department of Justice, Federal Bureau of Investigation, *Hate Crime Statistics, 2000*, https://ucr.fbi.gov/hate-crime/2000/hatecrime00.pdf; U.S. Department of Justice, Federal Bureau of Investigation, *Hate Crime Statistics, 2015*, https:// ucr.fbi.gov/hate-crime/2015.

19. Lu Ann Aday, "Health Status of Vulnerable Populations," *Annual Review, Public Health* 15 (1994): 487–509; Lu Ann Aday, *At Risk in America: The Health and Health Care Needs of Vulnerable Populations in the United States*, 2nd ed. (San Francisco: Jossey-Bass, 2001).

20. U.S. Department of Justice, Federal Bureau of Investigation, *Hate Crime Statistics, 2000*; U.S. Department of Justice, Federal Bureau of Investigation, *Hate Crime Statistics, 2015*.

21. Gordon W. Allport, *The Nature of Prejudice, 25th Anniversary Edition* (Cambridge, MA: Perseus Books, 1994), 191.

22. Allport, *Nature of Prejudice*, 192.

23. Rupert Brown, "Social Identity Theory: Past Achievements, Current Problems and Future Challenges," *European Journal of Social Psychology* 30 (2000): 745–78.

24. Yueh-Ting Lee, Lee J. Jussim, and Clark R. McCauley, "Why Study Stereotype Accuracy and Inaccuracy," in *Stereotyping Accuracy: Toward Appreciating Group Differences*, ed. Yueh-Ting Lee, Lee J. Jussim, and Clark R. McCauley (Washington, DC: American Psychological Association, 1995).

25. Domenico Montanaro, Danielle Kurtzleben, Scott Horsley, Sarah McCammon, and Richard Gonzales, "Fact Check: Donald Trump's Speech on Immigration," National Public Radio. August 31, 2016, http://www.npr.org/2016/08/31 /492096565/fact-check-donald-trumps-speech-on-immigration.

26. David Duke (@DrDavidDuke), Twitter, August 31, 2016, https://twitter .com/drdavidduke/status/771177837072048129?lang=en.

27. Richard Spencer (@RichardBSpencer), Twitter, August 31, 2016, https:// twitter.com/richardbspencer/status/771187277233922050.

28. Jared Taylor originally posted his tweet on August 31, 2016 (https://twitter .com/jartaylor?ref_src=twsrc%5Egoogle%7Ctwcamp%5Eserp%7Ctwgr%5

Eauthor). Since then, Twitter suspended Mr. Taylor's account. An account of Jared Taylor's tweet can be found at https://www.vox.com/2016/8/31/12744510/donald -trump-speech-white-nationalists.

29. Robin M. Williams Jr., *The Reduction of Intergroup Tensions: A Survey of Research on Problems of Ethnic, Racial, and Religious Group Relations* (New York: Social Science Research Council Bulletin, 1947), vol. 57, 143.

30. Allport, *Nature of Prejudice*, 195.

31. Paul M. Sniderman, Peri Pierangelo, Rui J. P. De Figueiredo Jr., and Thomas Piazza, *The Outsider: Prejudice and Politics in Italy* (Princeton, NJ: Princeton University Press, 2002).

32. Hubert M. Blalock Jr., *Toward a Theory of Minority-Group Relations* (New York: John Wiley & Sons, 1967).

33. Mark Hugo Lopez, *Modern Immigration Wave Brings 59 Million to U.S., Driving Population Growth and Change through 2065* (Washington, DC: Pew Research Center, 2015).

34. Tim Russert, "Rep. Luis Gutierrez (D-IL) and Pat Buchanan Debate Immigration Reform," *Meet the Press*, June 24, 2007, http://www.nbcnews.com/id /19354560/ns/meet_the_press/t/meet-press-transcript-june/#.WZio_yiGOUk.

35. Robert Short and Lisa Magana, "Political Rhetoric, Immigration Attitudes, and Contemporary Prejudice: A Mexican American Dilemma," *Journal of Social Psychology* 142, no. 6 (2002): 701–12.

36. Jennifer Jerit, "Survival of the Fittest: Rhetoric during the Course of an Election Campaign," *International Society of Political Psychology* 25, no. 4 (2004): 563–75.

37. Southern Poverty Law Center, *Hate Groups: State Totals*, https://www .splcenter.org/hate-map.

38. Southern Poverty Law Center, *Hate Map: National Numbers*, https://www .splcenter.org/hate-map.

39. Massimo Piatelli-Palmarini, *Inevitable Illusions: How Mistakes of Reason Rule Our Minds* (Hoboken, NJ: Wiley, 1994).

40. Blalock, *Toward a Theory of Minority-Group Relations*; Mikael Hjerm, "Do Numbers Really Count? Group Threat Theory Revisited," *Journal of Ethnic and Migration Studies* 33, no. 8 (2007): 1253–75; Ryan D. King and Darren Wheelock, "Group Threat and Social Control: Race, Perceptions of Minorities and the Desire to Punish," *Social Forces* 85, no. 3 (2007): 1255–80.

41. Allport, *The Nature of Prejudice*.

42. Blalock, *Toward a Theory of Minority-Group Relations*; Lawrence D. Bobo, "Prejudice as Group Position: Microfoundations of a Sociological Approach to Racism and Race Relations," *Journal of Social Issues* 55, no. 3 (1999): 445–72.

43. Michael W. Giles and Arthur Evans, "The Power Approach to Intergroup Hostility," *Journal of Conflict Resolution* 30, no. 3 (1986): 469–86; J. Eric Oliver and Janelle Wong, "Intergroup Prejudice in Multiethnic Settings," *American Journal of Political Science* 47, no. 4 (2003): 567–82; Elmar Schlueter and Peer Scheepers, "The Relationship between Out-Group Size and Anti-Out-Group Attitudes:

A Theoretical Synthesis and Empirical Test of Group Threat and Intergroup Contact Theory," *Social Science Research* 39 (2010): 285–95.

44. Lincoln Quillan, "Group Threat and Regional Change in Attitudes toward African-Americans," *American Journal of Sociology* 102, no. 3 (1996): 816–60.

45. Samuel P. Huntington, "The Hispanic Challenge," *Foreign Policy*, March /April 2004.

46. Ted Brader, Nicholas A. Valentino, and Elizabeth Suhay. 2008. "What Triggers Public Opposition to Immigration? Anxiety, Group Cues, and Immigration Threat," *American Journal of Political Science* 52, no. 4 (2008): 959–78.

47. Allport, *The Nature of Prejudice.*

48. Allport, *The Nature of Prejudice.*

49. Allport, *The Nature of Prejudice.*

50. Joseph G. Ponterotto, Shawn O. Utsey, and Paul Pedersen, *Preventing Prejudice: A Guide for Counselors, Educators, and Parents*, 2nd ed. (Thousand Oaks, CA: Sage, 2006).

51. Lawrence Bobo and Vincent L. Hutchings, "Perceptions of Racial Group Competition: Extending Blumer's Theory of Group Position to a Multiracial Social Context," *American Sociological Review* 61 (1996): 951–72.

52. National Geographic, *Inside the New Black Panthers (FULL part 1)*, July 27, 2011, https://www.youtube.com/watch?v=lEIsreNjN1E.

53. Josh Glasstetter, "Exclusive: Latinos Are Punch Line at Joe Arpaio Roast," Southern Poverty Law Center, February 26, 2014, https://www.splcenter.org /hatewatch/2014/02/26/exclusive-latinos-are-punch-line-joe-arpaio-roast.

54. Robert A. Levine and Donald T. Campbell, *Ethnocentrism* (New York: Wiley, 1972).

55. Levine and Campbell, *Ethnocentrism*; Muzafer Sherif, *Group Conflict and Co-Operation: Their Social Psychology* (London: Routledge and Kegan Paul, 1967).

56. Levine and Campbell, *Ethnocentrism*; Sherif, *Group Conflict and Co-Operation.*

57. Donald T. Campbell, "Ethnicentric and Other Altruistic Motives," D. Levine, ed., *Nebraska Symposium on Motivation* 13 (1965): 283–311; Sherif, *Group Conflict and Co-Operation.*

58. Sophie Gaudet and Richard Clément, "Forging an Identity as a Linguistic Minority: Intra-and Intergroup Aspects of Language, Communication and Identity in Western Canada," *International Journal of Intercultural Relations* 33, no. 3 (2009): 213–27.

59. George Knepper, *Ohio and Its People* (Kent, OH: Kent State University Press, 2003).

60. Donald P. Green, Laurence H. McFalls, and Jennifer K. Smith, "Hate Crime: An Empirical Research Agenda," *Annual Review of Sociology* 27 (2001): 479–504; Donald P. Green, Dara Z. Strolovitch, and Janelle S. Wong, "Defended Neighborhoods, Integration, and Racially Motivated Crime," *American Journal of Sociology* 104, no. 2 (1998): 372–403; Gerald D. Suttles, *The Social Construction of Communities* (Chicago: University of Chicago Press, 1972).

61. Robert E. Park, Ernest W. Burgess, and Roderick D. McKenzie, *The City* (Chicago: University of Chicago Press, 1967).

62. Green, Strolovitch, and Wong. "Defended Neighborhoods."

63. Kevin M. Kruse, *White Flight: Atlanta and the Making of Modern Conservatism* (Princeton, NJ: Princeton University Press, 2005).

64. Kruse, *White Flight*.

65. Dana D. Nelson, *National Citizenship: Capitalist Citizenship and the Imagined Fraternity of White Men* (Durham, NC: Duke University Press, 1998).

66. While the focus here is on microaggressions against minority groups by elected officials and the policies enacted by political elites, this research also acknowledges that microaggressions are not limited to one specific race or ethnic group, religion, or social class. Microaggressions occur within and among various minority groups and between minority and majority groups. Essentially, microaggressions are not always instigated by majority groups on minority groups. Underrepresented groups are also perpetrators of microaggressions.

67. Naomi Mandel, *Against the Unspeakable: Complicity, the Holocaust, and Slavery in America* (Charlottesville: University of Virginia Press, 2006), 169.

68. Feagin, *Racist America*.

69. Feagin, *Racist America*, 7.

70. Feagin, *Racist America*, 7.

71. Robert Pierce Forbes, *The Missouri Compromise and Its Aftermath: Slavery and the Meaning of America* (Chapel Hill: University of North Carolina Press, 2007).

72. Kenneth N. Addison, *"We Hold These Truths to be Self-Evident. . .": An Interdisciplinary Analysis of the Roots of Racism and Slavery in America* (Lanham, MD: University Press of America, 2009); Forbes, *The Missouri Compromise*; Mandel, *Against the Unspeakable*.

73. Eduardo Bonilla-Silva, *Racism without Racists*, 4th ed. (Lanham, MD: Rowman and Littlefield, 2014), 3.

74. William N. Eskridge Jr., "Is Political Powerlessness a Requirement for Heightened Equal Protection Scrutiny?" Yale Law School Faculty Scholarship Series, Paper 3780 (2010), 18, http://digitalcommons.law.yale.edu/fss_papers/3780/.

75. Douglas S. Massey and Nancy A. Denton, *American Apartheid: Segregation and the Making of the Underclass* (Cambridge, MA: Harvard University Press, 1998).

76. Eskridge, "Is Political Powerlessness a Requirement?" 18.

77. Feagin, *Racist America*.

78. Earl Warren, *The Memoirs of Earl Warren* (New York: Doubleday, 1977), 291–92.

79. Warren, *Memoirs of Earl Warren*, 291–92.

80. Michael J. Klarman, *From Jim Crow to Civil Rights: The Supreme Court and the Struggle for Racial Equality* (Oxford: Oxford University Press, 2004).

81. Kruse, *White Flight*.

82. "W.Va. Mayor Resigns for Response to Racist Comments about Michelle Obama," Associated Press, November 15, 2016, https://www.bostonglobe.com/news/nation/2016/11/15/official-leave-after-posting-racist-comments-about-michelle-obama/xbEoQYihgK60WuHGjtiWjM/story.html.

83. Graham Smith, *When Jim Crow Met John Bull: Black American Soldiers in World War II Britain* (London: I.B. Tauris, 1987).

84. "Michelle Obama," https://www.whitehouse.gov/about-the-white-house/first-ladies/michelle-obama/.

85. Allport, *Nature of Prejudice*.

86. Allport, *Nature of Prejudice*.

87. U.S. Census Bureau, American Fact Finder, https://factfinder.census.gov/faces/nav/jsf/pages/community_facts.xhtml.

88. Sandra L. Colby and Jennifer M. Ortman, *Projections of the Size and Composition of the U.S. Population: 2014 to 2060.* (Washington, DC: U.S. Census Bureau, 2014).

89. Colby and Ortman, *Projections of the Size and Composition of the U.S. Population*.

90. Shirley Hune, "Politics of Chinese Exclusion: Legislative-Executive Conflict 1876–1882," in *Asian Americans and the Law Historical and Contemporary Perspectives*, series ed. Charles McClain (New York: Garland, 1994), 93–116.

91. Andrew Gyory, "Chinese Exclusion Acts," in *Encyclopedia of U.S. Labor and Working-Class History, Volume 1 A-F Index*, ed. Eric Arnesen (New York: Routledge, 2007), 240–41.

92. Leila Higgins, "Immigration and the Vulnerable Worker: We Built This Country on Cheap Labor," *Labor & Employment Law Forum* 3, no. 3 (2013): 522–59.

93. Congressional Globe, 39th Cong., 1st Sess., https://memory.loc.gov/ammem/amlaw/lwcglink.html#anchor39, 1056.

94. Chinese Exclusion Act, 1882, *Statutes at Large*, vol. 22, sec 1–14: 58.

95. Ashley Killough and Tom LoBianco, "Trump Slams Bush for Tying Asians to 'Anchor Babies,'" CNN, August 25, 2015, http://www.cnn.com/2015/08/24/politics/jeb-bush-asian-people-anchor-babies/.

96. Williams Jr., *Reduction of Intergroup Tensions*.

97. Lopez, *Modern Immigration Wave*.

98. Jeffrey S. Passel and D'Vera Cohn, *Unauthorized Immigrant Population: National and State Trends 2010* (Washington DC: Pew Hispanic Center, 2011), 1–31; Michael Hoefer, Nancy Rytina, and Bryan C. Baker, *Estimates of the Unauthorized Immigrant Population Residing in the United States: January 2007* (Washington, DC: Office of Immigration Statistics, 2008); Michael Hoefer, Nancy Rytina and Bryan C. Baker, *Estimates of the Unauthorized Immigrant Population Residing in the United States: January 2008* (Washington, DC: Office of Immigration Statistics, 2009); Michael Hoefer, Nancy Rytina and Bryan C. Baker, *Estimates of the Unauthorized Immigrant Population Residing in the United States: January 2009* (Washington, DC: Office of Immigration Statistics, 2010); Robert Warren and John Robert Warren, "Unauthorized Immigration to the United States: Annual Estimates and Components of Change, by State, 1990 to 2010," *International Migration Review* 47, no. 2 (2013): 296–329.

99. Hoefer, Rytina, and Baker, "Estimates of the Unauthorized Immigrant Population Residing in the United States: January 2007"; Hoefer, Rytina, and

Baker, "Estimates of the Unauthorized Immigrant Population Residing in the United States: January 2008"; Hoefer, Rytina, and Baker, "Estimates of the Unauthorized Immigrant Population Residing in the United States: January 2009"; Passel and Cohn, *Unauthorized Immigrant Population*, 1–31.

100. Kevin Johnson, "The New Nativism: Something Old, Something New, Something Borrowed, Something Blue," in *Immigrants Out! The New Nativism and the Anti-Immigrant Impulse in the United States*, ed. J.F. Perea (New York: New York University Press, 1997), 165–89; George Sanchez, "Face the Nation: Race, Immigration and the Rise of Nativism in Late Twentieth Century America," *International Migration Review* 31, no. 4 (1997): 1009–30.

101. Joe R. Feagin and José A. Cobas, *Latinos Facing Racism: Discrimination, Resistance and Endurance* (New York: Routledge, 2016), 1–2.

102. Donald J. Trump @realDonaldTrump), Twitter, July 13, 2015, https://twitter.com/realdonaldtrump/status/620546522556534784?lang=en.

103. Joe R. Feagin, "White Supremacy and Mexican Americans: Rethinking the "Black-White Paradigm," *Rutgers Law Review* 54 (Summer 2002).

104. Richard Griswold Del Castillo, *The Treaty of Guadalupe Hidalgo: A Legacy of Conflict* (Norman: University of Oklahoma Press, 1990).

105. John C. Calhoun, Speech on the Conquest of Mexico on the Floor of the Senate, 1848, http://teachingamericanhistory.org/library/document/speech-on-the-mexican-american-war/.

106. "Gov. Brewer: AZ 'Has Been under Terrorist Attack. . .with All This Illegal Immigration," Fox News, https://www.youtube.com/watch?v=w8EKhl4-bCA.

107. Cassie Miller and Alexandra Werner-Winslow, *Ten Days After: Harassment and Intimidation in the Aftermath of the Election*, Southern Poverty Law Center, November 29, 2016, https://www.splcenter.org/20161129/ten-days-after-harassment-and-intimidation-aftermath-election.

108. Miller and Werner-Winslow, *Ten Days After.*

109. *The 9/11 Commission Report* (New York: W.W. Norton, 2004).

110. *The 9/11 Commission Report*, 1–2.

111. U.S. Department of Justice, Federal Bureau of Investigation, *Hate Crime Statistics, 2001*, https://ucr.fbi.gov/hate-crime/2001/hatecrime01.pdf.

112. Katayoun Kishi, "Anti-Muslim Assaults Reach 9/11 Era Levels, FBI Data Show," Pew Research Center, November 21, 2016, http://www.pewresearch.org/fact-tank/2016/11/21/anti-muslim-assaults-reach-911-era-levels-fbi-data-show/.

113. Mark Potok, "The Trump Effect," *Intelligence Report* (Spring 2007), https://www.splcenter.org/fighting-hate/intelligence-report/2017/trump-effect.

114. Potok, "The Trump Effect."

115. "Executive Order Protecting the Nation from Foreign Terrorist Entry into the United States," March 6, 2017, https://www.whitehouse.gov/the-press-office/2017/03/06/executive-order-protecting-nation-foreign-terrorist-entry-united-states

116. Julia Jacobo, "32-Year-Old Man Arrested in Connection to Arson at Florida Mosque, Police Say," ABC News, September 14, 2016, http://abcnews.go.com/US/32-year-man-arrested-connection-arson-florida-mosque/story?id=42098425.

117. Derek Hawkins, "Man Accused of Fla. Mosque Arson Has Multiple Convictions, Served Time for Theft," *Washington Post*, September 15, 2016, https://www.washingtonpost.com/news/morning-mix/wp/2016/09/15/accused-fla-mosque-arsonist-has-multiple-convictions-served-time-for-theft/?utm_term=.06336a2b1e8b.

118. Julie Zauzmer, "'Muslim Piece of Trash': D.C. Police Investigating Possible Hate Crime Outside a Coffee Shop," *Washington Post*, May 2, 2016, https://www.washingtonpost.com/news/acts-of-faith/wp/2016/05/02/muslim-piece-of-trash-d-c-police-investigating-possible-hate-crime-outside-a-coffee-shop/?utm_term=.c1309313c287. A video of the assault can be viewed at https://www.washingtonpost.com/video/local/police-looking-for-assault-suspect-in-possible-hate-crime-outside-dc-coffee-shop/2016/05/02/cb2ff294-10d0-11e6-a9b5-bf703a5a7191_video.html.

## Chapter 5: The Realization That Times Are Changing

1. Julie Zauzmer, "'Muslim Piece of Trash': D.C. Police Investigating Possible Hate Crime Outside a Coffee Shop," *Washington Post*, May 2, 2016, https://www.washingtonpost.com/news/acts-of-faith/wp/2016/05/02/muslim-piece-of-trash-d-c-police-investigating-possible-hate-crime-outside-a-coffee-shop/?utm_term=.c1309313c287. A video of the assault can be viewed at https://www.washingtonpost.com/video/local/police-looking-for-assault-suspect-in-possible-hate-crime-outside-dc-coffee-shop/2016/05/02/cb2ff294-10d0-11e6-a9b5-bf703a5a7191_video.html.

2. Sandra L. Colby and Jennifer M. Ortman, *Projections of the Size and Composition of the U.S. Population: 2014 to 2060* (Washington, DC: U.S. Census Bureau, 2014).

3. Colby and Ortman, *Projections of the Size and Composition of the U.S. Population*.

4. D'Vera Cohn and Andrea Caumont, "10 Demographic Trends That Are Shaping the U.S. and the World," Pew Research Center, March 31, 2016, http://www.pewresearch.org/fact-tank/2016/03/31/10-demographic-trends-that-are-shaping-the-u-s-and-the-world/.

5. Here the term *Anglo-Protestant* is used to align with Samuel Huntington's use of the term in "The Hispanic Challenge" (*Foreign Policy*, March/April 2004) and in *Who Are We? The Challenges to America's National Identity* (New York: Simon & Schuster, 2004).

6. Take, for example, the Carter, Reagan, and Clinton administrations that severely cut funding to programs that directly impact groups that are disadvantaged.

7. For example, job creation, reducing the cost of higher education, funding for job training, increasing minimum wages, and affordable house.

8. Wen Ho Lee, *My Country Versus Me* (New York: Hyperion, 2001), 251–52.

9. Lee has not been the only Chinese American falsely accused of espionage. See the cases of Xiaxing Xi, a professor of physics at Temple University; Sherry Chen, a hydrologist for the National Weather Service; and Guoqing Cao and Shuyu Li, senior biologists at Eli Lilly.

10. American National Elections Studies, *The ANES Guide to Public Opinion and Electoral Behavior* (Ann Arbor: University of Michigan, Center for Political Studies and Stanford University, 2017).

11. American National Elections Studies, *The ANES Guide.*

12. Paul Spickard, *Japanese Americans The Formation and Transformation of an Ethnic Group*, rev ed. (New Brunswick, NJ: Rutgers University Press, 2009), 107.

13. See the following tweets by Donald Trump (@realDonaldTrump): May 18, 2012, https://twitter.com/realDonaldTrump/status/203568571148800001; May 30, 2012, https://twitter.com/realDonaldTrump/status/207875027008368640; August 6, 2012, https://twitter.com/realDonaldTrump/status/2325725052384 33794; December 12, 2013, https://twitter.com/realDonaldTrump/status/4112 47268763676673; November 23, 2014, https://twitter.com/realDonaldTrump /status/536653754029047808.

14. "Exclusive: Donald Trump Rips Into President Obama's Past," *Hannity*, Fox News, April 15, 2011, http://www.foxnews.com/transcript/2011/04/15/exclusive -donald-trump-rips-into-president-obama-past.html.

15. Eduardo Bonilla-Silva, *Racism without Racists*, 4th ed. (Lanham, MD: Rowman and Littlefield, 2014), 4.

16. Bonilla-Silva, *Racism without Racists*, 4.

17. Howard Schuman, Charlotte Steeh, and Lawrence Bobo, *Racial Attitudes in America: Trends and Interpretations* (Cambridge, MA: Harvard University Press, 1985), 73–81.

18. Schuman, Steeh, and Bobo, *Racial Attitudes in America.*

19. Pew Research Center, *On Views of Race and Inequality, Blacks and Whites Are Worlds Apart*, June 27, 2016, http://assets.pewresearch.org/wp-content/uploads /sites/3/2016/06/ST_2016.06.27_Race-Inequality-Final.pdf.

20. Pew Research Center, *On Views of Race and Inequality.*

21. Pew Research Center, *On Views of Race and Inequality.*

22. Pew Research Center, *On Views of Race and Inequality*, 6.

23. Pew Research Center, *On Views of Race and Inequality*, 7.

24. Paul B. Sheatsley, "White Attitudes toward the Negro," in *The Negro American*, ed. Talcott Parsons and Kenneth B. Clark (Boston: Beacon, 1966), 323.

25. "1978 Speech by Gingrich," *Frontline: The Long March of Newt Gingrich*, http://www.pbs.org/wgbh/pages/frontline/newt/newt78speech.html.

## Chapter 6: Trump: Unconventionality in the White House

1. Donald J. Trump @realDonaldTrump), Twitter, July 16, 2015, https:// twitter.com/realDonaldTrump/status/621783757532626944.

2. Donald J. Trump @realDonaldTrump), Twitter, August 15, 2015, https://twitter.com/realDonaldTrump/status/630455091091374080.

3. Donald J. Trump @realDonaldTrump), Twitter, July 16, 2015, https://twitter.com/realDonaldTrump/status/621781334592241665

4. Donald J. Trump @realDonaldTrump), Twitter, November 22, 2017, https://twitter.com/realDonaldTrump/status/933280234220134401.

5. Arlie Russell Hochschild, *Strangers in Their Own Land: Anger and Mourning on the American Right* (New York: New Press, 2016).

6. Hochschild, *Strangers in Their Own Land*; "What Drives Trump Supporters?: Sociologist Arlie Russell Hochschild on Anger & Mourning of the Right—Part One," *Democracy Now*, September 28, 2016, https://www.democracynow.org/2016/9/28/what_drives_trump_supporters_sociologist_arlie.

7. Hochschild, *Strangers in Their Own Land*, 146.

8. Hochschild, *Strangers in Their Own Land*, 146.

9. Hochschild, *Strangers in Their Own Land*, 222.

10. Hochschild, *Strangers in Their Own Land*, 225.

11. Hochschild, "What Drives Trump Supporters?"

12. Robert B. Reich, *Saving Capitalism: For The Many, Not The Few* (New York: Vintage Books, 2016), 187–88.

13. For the complete version of Professor de la Garza's comments, see Danielle Kurtzleben, "'Politics Has Become Celebrity-Driven': How 2016 Surprised Political Thinkers," National Public Radio, July 17, 2016, https://www.npr.org/2016/07/17/484016283/-politics-has-become-celebrity-driven-how-2016-surprised-political-thinkers.

14. Michael Barber and Jeremy C. Pope, "Does Party Trump Ideology? Disentangling Party and Ideology in America," https://www.dropbox.com/s/jo4kq5g24zpz0zs/Does_Party_Trump_Ideology_.pdf?dl=0.

15. Barber and Pope, "Does Party Trump Ideology?"

16. In the 2016 U.S. presidential election one of Trump's campaign slogans was "Make America Great Again."

17. See RealClear Politics, Direction of Country Poll, Polling Data, https://www.realclearpolitics.com/epolls/other/direction_of_country-902.html; Mark Murray, "Trump's Approval Rating Drops to Lowest Level Yet in New NBC News /WSJ Poll," NBC News, October 29, 2017, https://www.nbcnews.com/politics /donald-trump/trump-s-approval-rating-drops-lowest-level-yet-new-nbc -n815321; Jennifer Hansler, "Trump's Approval Rating Hits Historic Low, Washington Post-ABC Poll Says," CNN, November 6, 2017, http://www.cnn.com /2017/11/05/politics/wapo-abc-poll-nov-5/index.html; "Presidential Approval Ratings—Donald Trump," Gallup, http://news.gallup.com/poll/203198/presi dential-approval-ratings-donald-trump.aspx.

18. The Russian government was successful in influencing the 2016 U.S. presidential election by using social media (Google, Facebook, and Twitter) to negatively portray Democratic candidate Hillary Clinton and to post false information regarding the candidate. Also, refer to "CIA Director Keynote Remarks," C-SPAN,

July 11, 2017, https://www.c-span.org/video/?431113-1/cia-director-says-russia -clearly-meddled-2016-election.

19. "CIA Director Keynote Remarks."

20. See Office of the Director of National Intelligence, *Assessing Russian Activities and Intentions in Recent U.S. Elections*, January 6, 2017, https://www.intelli gence.senate.gov/sites/default/files/documents/ICA_2017_01.pdf; and U.S. Senate Select Committee on Intelligence, *Report to Accompany S.1761, The Intelligence Authorization Act for Fiscal Year 2018 (September 7, 2017)*, Sections 609–612, 613– 615, S. Rpt. 115–151, https://www.intelligence.senate.gov/publications/report -accompany-s1761-intelligence-authorization-act-fiscal-year-2018-septem ber-7-2017.

21. Donald J. Trump @realDonaldTrump), Twitter, August 7, 2017, https:// twitter.com/realdonaldtrump/status/894525428236464128?lang=en.

22. Donald J. Trump @realDonaldTrump), Twitter, August 15, 2017, https:// twitter.com/realdonaldtrump/status/897411177583702016?lang=en.

23. Donald J. Trump @realDonaldTrump), Twitter, September 22, 2017, https://twitter.com/realdonaldtrump/status/911179462745710593?lang=en.

24. Donald J. Trump @realDonaldTrump), Twitter, October 29, 2017, https:// twitter.com/realdonaldtrump/status/924649059520073730?lang=en.

25. Donald J. Trump @realDonaldTrump), Twitter, October 29, 2017, https:// twitter.com/realdonaldtrump/status/924637600094326784?lang=en.

26. Julie Hirschfield Davis, "Trump Says Putin 'Means It' about Not Meddling," *New York Times*, November 11, 2017, https://www.nytimes.com/2017/11 /11/world/asia/trump-putin-election.html.

27. Ben Sasse, "An Open Letter to Trump Supporters," Facebook, February 28, 2016, https://www.facebook.com/sassefornebraska/posts/593031420862025.

28. For the complete version of Senator Corker's interview, see "Corker: Leaders Know What Trump Says Is Untrue," CNN, October 24, 2017, http://www .cnn.com/videos/politics/2017/10/24/bob-corker-on-trump-intv-raju-nr.cnn /video/playlists/sen-bob-corker/.

29. For the complete version of John McCain's op-ed, see "John McCain: It's Time Congress Returns to Regular Order," *Washington Post*, August 31, 2017, https://www.washingtonpost.com/opinions/john-mccain-its-time-congress -returns-to-regular-order/2017/08/31/f62a3e0c-8cfb-11e7-8df5-c2e5cf46c1e2 _story.html?utm_term=.a62526bb4353.

30. For the complete version of Senator Flake's speech, see "Senator Jeff Flake Won't Seek Re-election, Condemns President Trump's Behavior," C-SPAN, October 24, 2017, https://www.c-span.org/video/?c4687651/senator-jeff-flake-wont -seek-re-election-condemns-president-trumps-behavior.

31. "Remarks by President George W. Bush and Mrs. Laura Bush at the 'Spirit of Liberty: At Home, In The World,'" October 19, 2017, https://www.bushcenter .org/about-the-center/newsroom/press-releases/2017/10/gwb-lwb-spirit-of -liberty-remarks.html.

32. "Remarks by President George W. Bush."

## Chapter 7: The Transformation Process and the Challenges Ahead

1. Steve King (@SteveKingIA), Twitter, March 12, 2017, https://twitter.com/SteveKingIA?ref_src=twsrc%5Egoogle%7Ctwcamp%5Eserp%7Ctwgr%5Eauthor.

2. Alissa J. Rubin, "Geert Wilders, Reclusive Provocateur, Rises before Dutch Vote," *New York Times*, February 27, 2017, https://www.nytimes.com/2017/02/27/world/europe/geert-wilders-reclusive-provocateur-rises-before-dutch-vote.html.

3. Geert Wilders (@geertwilderspv), "Wilders: Defend Our Freedom" YouTube, April 21, 2017, https://www.youtube.com/watch?v=dm5w8k1hyzk&feature=youtu.be. And, posted to Facebook on June 4, 2017 https://www.facebook.com/geertwilders/posts/376034999461440.

4. David Duke (@DrDavidDuke), Twitter, March 12, 2017, https://twitter.com/DrDavidDuke/status/841006623262986241.

5. Maureen Groppe, "What Trump Has Said about Judge Curiel," IndyStar, June 11, 2016, https://www.indystar.com/story/news/2016/06/11/what-trump-has-said-judge-curiel/85641242/v.

6. Jake Tapper, "Donald Trump Rails against Judge's 'Mexican Heritage,'" CNN, June 3, 2016, http://www.cnn.com/videos/politics/2016/06/03/donald-trump-judge-mexican-trump-university-case-lead-sot.cnn.

7. Rebecca Shabad, "Paul Ryan: Donald Trump's Remarks on Judge Are 'Textbook Definition of a Racist Comment,'" CBS News, June 7, 2016, https://www.cbsnews.com/news/paul-ryan-donald-trumps-remarks-on-judge-are-textbook-definition-of-a-racist-comment/.

8. "Gingrich: Trump Remarks about Judge 'Mistake,' 'Inexcusable,'" Fox News, June 5, 2016, http://www.foxnews.com/politics/2016/06/05/gingrich-trump-remarks-about-judge-mistake-inexcusable.html.

9. Sally Bronston, "McConnell on Trump Judge Comments: 'I Couldn't Disagree More,'" *Meet the Press*, June 5, 2016, http://www.nbcnews.com/meet-the-press/mcconnell-trump-judge-comments-i-couldn-t-disagree-more-n586056.

10. Herbert Blumer, "Race Prejudice as a Sense of Group Position," *Pacific Sociological Review* 1, no. 1 (1958): 3–7.

11. Chester M. Pierce, Jean V. Carew, Diane Pierce-Gonzalez, and Deborah Wills, "An Experiment in Racism: TV Commercials," *Sage Contemporary, Social Science Issues* 44 (1978): 62–88.

12. "Remarks by President George W. Bush and Mrs. Laura Bush at the 'Spirit of Liberty: At Home, In The World,'" October 19, 2017, https://www.bushcenter.org/about-the-center/newsroom/press-releases/2017/10/gwb-lwb-spirit-of-liberty-remarks.html.

13. See Eduardo Bonilla-Silva, *Racism without Racists*, 4th ed. (New York: Rowman & Littlefield, 2014), 302–3.

14. See Rodney O. Davis and Douglas L. Wilson, eds. *The Lincoln-Douglas Debates* (Galesburg, Il: Knox College Lincoln Studies Center; Urbana: University of Illinois Press, 2008), 19.

15. See Davis and Wilson, *Lincoln-Douglas Debates*, 20.

16. At the time of the first debate Lincoln had considered freeing slaves and sending them back to Liberia. At other points in time, Lincoln had also considered colonization where slaves would be freed and encouraged to leave the United States. It was not until the Emancipation Proclamation that Lincoln explicitly called for all slaves to be freed. Refer to Eric Foner, *The Fiery Trial: Abraham Lincoln and American Slavery* (New York: W.W. Norton, 2010).

17. American National Elections Studies, *The ANES Guide to Public Opinion and Electoral Behavior* (Ann Arbor: University of Michigan, Center for Political Studies and Stanford University, 2017).

18. American National Elections Studies, *The ANES Guide.*

19. "1978 Speech by Gingrich," *Frontline: The Long March of Newt Gingrich*, http://www.pbs.org/wgbh/pages/frontline/newt/newt78speech.html.

20. Bonilla-Silva, *Racism without Racists*, 15.

# Index

## About the Author

**Sylvia Gonzalez-Gorman, PhD**, is an assistant professor at the University of Texas Rio Grande Valley, Brownsville, Texas. Her current areas of interest are Latino politics, immigration, state and local government, urban and local affairs, and public policy.